EMPLOYER'S ATTITUDES TOWARDS PEOPLE WITH DISABILITIES

Sheila Honey, Nigel Meager
and Matthew Williams

INSTITUTE OF MANPOWER STUDIES

Manpower Commentary Series

Report 245

Published by:

INSTITUTE OF MANPOWER STUDIES

at the University of Sussex

Mantell Building
Falmer
Brighton BN1 9RF
UK

Tel. 0273 686751
Fax 0273 690430

Manpower Commentary No. 54
Copyright © 1993 Institute of Manpower Studies

A catalogue record for this book is available from the British Library

ISBN 1-85184-168-7

Printed in Great Britain by College Hill Press Ltd

EMPLOYER'S ATTITUDES TOWARDS PEOPLE WITH DISABILITIES

The Institute of Manpower Studies

The Institute of Manpower Studies is an independent, international centre of research and consultancy in human resource issues. It has close working contacts with employers in the manufacturing, service and public sectors, government departments, agencies, professional and employee bodies, and foundations. Since it was established over 20 years ago the Institute has been a focus of knowledge and practical experience in employment and training policy, the operation of labour markets and human resource planning and development. IMS is a not-for-profit organisation which has a multidisciplinary staff of over 50. IMS expertise is available to all organisations through research, consultancy, training and publications.

The Manpower Commentary Programme

The IMS Manpower Commentary is produced on behalf of the Employment Department. The Institute of Manpower Studies has conducted research under this remit continuously since 1976, on a range of manpower topics which are of interest to the Department, thereby usefully complementing the ED Group's own research effort. Specifically, the remit requires the Institute to produce a regular, independent commentary on issues affecting manpower policy, drawing particularly on information which the Institute derives from its work with companies.

The scope of the Commentary is to report on the impact of Government policy and of current and emerging trends in the labour market on firms' employment policies and practices; firms reactions to changes in the availability and mobility of particular kinds of labour; ways in which the effectiveness of companies' use of manpower could be improved; and the impact on groups of individuals of trends in employment. Additional relevant subjects for inclusion in the Commentary may be requested by the Department from time to time.

A joint Liaison Committee, composed of ED representatives and Institute staff, monitors this activity. The Group is required to give consideration to the use of funds and the development of the Commentary Programme. The Liaison Committee accordingly agrees the scope of the successive issues of the Manpower Commentary, and receives them on behalf of the ED Group.

The views expressed in this report are those of the authors and may not necessarily reflect those of the Employment Department

Contents

Executive Summary

Introduction (chapter 1)

This Commentary presents the results of a study commissioned by the Employment Department, of current practice in the employment of people with disabilities.

The object of the research was to provide Government with a clearer picture than that currently available of:

● employers' policies towards recruiting and employing people with disabilities;

● what employers currently do, what they do not feel able to do, and why; and

● what kinds of help and assistance employers need if they are to be able to do more in this area.

The research consisted of three main elements:

● an extensive review of previous research in this area[1];

● a postal survey of employers to establish the current extent of recruitment and employment of people with disabilities. This consisted of a core sample of 1,855 randomly chosen organisations. A further 351 'good practice' organisations were also surveyed to act as a control group. The survey achieved an overall response rate of 52 per cent;

● in–depth case studies of 21 employers, pursuing in greater detail issues arising in the recruitment, employment and retention of employees with disabilities. These were selected to represent a broad spread across size and sector, and to represent those employing/not employing disabled people and those with positive/negative attitudes as expressed in questionnaire responses.

The employment of people with disabilities (chapter 2)

This chapter looks in broad terms at whether employers have employees with disabilities, and how this varies by size and sector; the extent to which employees with disabilities were registered as

---

[1]   This review is summarised in Appendix 3 below.

disabled; and the main types of disability which were found in the organisations in question.

Extent of employment of people with disabilities

Just over half of responding organisations replied that they employed people with disabilities. As expected, there were considerable differences between the random sub–sample and the 'good practice' sub–sample (49 per cent of the former having employees with disabilities compared with 92 per cent of the latter).

Variation by size

Size was revealed to be a more important influence than sector on whether or not organisations employ people with disabilities. The likelihood of employing disabled workers increases consistently with size. Only 15 per cent of organisations with ten employees or fewer employ people with disabilities, whilst all organisations with over 5,000 employees have disabled workers.

Variation by sector

For the sample as a whole, production organisations are much more likely than average to employ people with disabilities. Three quarters of organisations in the metals and minerals sector and almost nine out of ten energy and water supply organisations employ disabled workers. By contrast, 44 per cent of construction sector organisations and only 40 per cent of those in transport and communication employ people with disabilities. More detailed analysis suggests, however, that much of this apparent sectoral variation was due to the different average size of organisations in the different sectors.

Disabled employees' share of the workforce

The survey found that employees with disabilities comprise less than three per cent of the workforce in over a half of responding organisations. Registered disabled employees make up a much smaller proportion of the workforce, accounting for less than three per cent of employees in almost nine out of ten organisations. Although the three per cent quota applies only to organisations with 20 or more employees, the results confirm that across all size bands it is only a small minority of organisations that meet the quota for registered disabled employees. Taking the combined workforce of all respondents, the proportion of disabled employees is 1.3 per cent, while the proportion of registered disabled workers is 0.6 per cent.

Incidence of different disability types

By far the most common types of disability are those related to mobility, and more than three quarters of organisations reported these disabilities among their employees. The next most common types were hearing, seeing problems, diabetes and chest or breathing problems, each of which were cited by between 40 and 50 per cent of respondents. Least common were blood disorders, reported by fewer than one in eight respondents.

2

There was some sectoral variation in the different types of disability found amongst employees. Thus, for example, the construction sector was least likely to employ people with mobility problems, whilst the financial and business services and other services were more likely than average to employ people with sight problems.

Organisations not employing people with disabilities (chapter 3)

This chapter singles out the 42 per cent of organisations who do not employ people with disabilities, looking at the reasons for this, as well as any problems or difficulties which these organisations saw as being associated with the recruitment, employment or retention of people with disabilities.

Reasons for non–employment of people with disabilities

Just over three quarters of respondents to this question indicated that they did not employ people with disabilities, simply because no–one with a disability had applied for employment, although in a number of case studies respondents stressed that some disabled people might have applied but not identified themselves as such to the employer. The other main reason given was that the organisation had employed people with disabilities in the past but they had subsequently left. This, however, accounted for only 19 per cent of respondents to this question.

Very few of these organisations (20 out of 482) stated that they had not recruited a person with a disability because their disability was a barrier for a particular job. The sector in which this was most common was transport and communications, with nine per cent giving this reason.

Perceived problems associated with disabled employees

Respondents to the survey who did not employ people with disabilities were asked if they associated particular problems with the employment of disabled people, to which 68 per cent answered that they did. Interestingly there was little variation in this propensity by employment size and a rather greater variation by sector — with construction sector employers being most likely to associate employment of people with disabilities with particular difficulties/ problems (90 per cent said they would), and business services and other manufacturing least likely to do so.

The source of difficulty most frequently cited was related to the types of work or jobs the organisation could offer to people with disabilities. This option was cited by 77 per cent, particularly in organisations with a high proportion of manual occupations, and was often linked to the 'physically demanding' nature of the work, or to health and safety issues. The next three most common sources of difficulty were related to the nature of the organisation's premises or physical environment.

Further questioning during the case studies suggested that many of these perceived difficulties are associated with stereotypical views of the range of disabilities likely to be encountered in the population at large (*eg* there was a common association among respondents between 'disability' and wheelchair use). These are organisations which did not employ people with disabilities, however, and the case studies also suggested that organisations who had themselves encountered a wide range of disabilities had a much broader image of disabled people, and were much less likely to think of stereotypical examples in discussing such issues.

This group of respondents were also asked if they felt there were any particular problems or difficulties associated with the *retention of existing employees* who have become disabled. Twenty eight per cent of respondents felt there would be such problems, whilst 35 per cent said that there would not. The key point is that even among organisations which did not employ people with disabilities, attitudes towards the retention of existing employees who become disabled are considerably more positive than those towards the employment of people with disabilities in general.

Employers' policies towards people with disabilities (chapter 4)

This chapter examines whether or not organisations have policies on the recruitment and employment of people with disabilities, and the nature of these policies, with particular emphasis on the approach taken towards recruiting people with disabilities.

Incidence of policies

Fewer than half of the organisations responding to the survey had a policy relating to the employment of people with disabilities (a quarter had a written policy and the remaining 19 per cent said it was unwritten).

Variation with size

As expected, size of organisation was a strong influence on whether a written policy had been introduced. Only 9.5 per cent of companies in the smallest size band had a policy at all and only 2.9 per cent had written it down. The proportions of those with a policy, both written and unwritten, rose with increasing size. Having said this, only half of the organisations employing between 500 and 4,999 employees had a written policy, and even in the largest organisations (5,000 or more employees) there were still a few organisations without a policy. Unsurprisingly, organisations employing people with disabilities were more likely to have a policy that those who did not.

Scope of, and rationale for policies

The scope of policies and the motivations for introducing them were followed up in some detail in the case studies. Most case study organisations saw disability as an equal opportunities issue, and as such, policies on the employment of people with disabilities tended to be integrated into their more general equal opportunity policies. All organisations with a policy on disability said that it covered all aspects of employment, not just recruitment.

Monitoring of policies

Ensuring the implementation of the equal opportunities policy relies on some sort of monitoring processes being undertaken. Monitoring processes depend very much on the size of the organisation. Those employing fewer than 200 staff tend to adopt an *ad hoc* approach to implementation and monitoring: *'the company is small enough and we know what is going on'*.

Generally, the largest organisations interviewed had more formal methods of monitoring, such as asking questions regarding health *etc.* on application forms. Several interviewees felt, however, that some individuals may not admit to having a disability on an application form and so the numbers of disabled people in the recruitment process are likely to be underestimated. Some organisations had removed such questions (as part of an equal opportunities policy, to avoid disability being used by managers as a screening criterion), but this effectively prevented them from operating a 'Guaranteed Interview Scheme'. Monitoring existing employees for disability was also seen as a difficult area due to the reluctance of some staff to identify themselves as disabled since they saw it *'as some form of threat or as limiting their chances of career progression'*.

Implementation of policies on disability in employment

Policy implementation was seen as a difficult issue by most personnel managers in the case study organisations. In small organisations they tended to rely on the personnel manager being aware personally of what was going on. When organisations were too large for central personnel staff to be involved in all recruitment and selection, the majority provided managers with training in selection techniques including equal opportunity and disability issues, and ensured individual staff were informed of their organisation's equal opportunities policy and of the mechanisms for complaint.

Active recruitment of people with disabilities

Organisations were also asked in the questionnaire whether they actively sought to recruit people with disabilities, the methods they used in doing so, and the vacancies to which this policy applied. Only one in five respondents said they were actively seeking to recruit people with disabilities. Once again, the proportion with active recruitment policies in this sense increased strongly with organisation size. Whether organisations already employed people with disabilities was also an important factor. Of those that had disabled employees, 32 per cent said they were actively seeking to recruit more. Among organisations which had no employees with disabilities, the proportion was only five per cent.

Although this may appear to suggest a negative outlook for the recruitment of people with disabilities, in that few organisations were active in the recruitment of people with disabilities, this is not necessarily a reflection of antipathy towards disability issues. Comments from both the questionnaires and case studies indicate that many organisations would be keen to do more, but are unable to do so at present due to low or static levels of recruitment in the recession.

Methods of recruitment of people with disabilities

Among those organisations actively seeking to recruit people with disabilities, nearly half indicated that they did this for all vacancies. Very few organisations with a pro–active recruitment strategy limited recruiting people with disabilities to a specified range of vacancies. The questionnaire also examined how such organisations went about attracting job applicants with disabilities. The two most frequently used methods were job advertisements welcoming disabled applicants, and notification of vacancies to the Employment Service disability specialists, both of which approaches were used by approximately half of these respondents. A third of respondents who actively recruited disabled people (nearly all from the 'good practice' sub–sample) used the Employment Service disability symbol in their literature.

The case studies confirmed that although most organisations did approach either Jobcentres or use the ES services in this context, there was a wide range of other methods being employed, such as open days, recruitment fairs and establishing links with disability organisations. Many organisations had also revised their general recruitment practices, *eg* by training all recruitment staff in equal opportunity issues; revising application forms and using new employee starter forms; drawing up much tighter job descriptions and person specifications; operating guaranteed interview schemes and offering work experience and training schemes.

The pros and cons of employing people with disabilities (chapter 5)

This chapter looks at the benefits seen by employers as associated with the employment of people with disabilities, and at any problems and difficulties employers perceive in recruiting and employing disabled people. It should be stressed (particularly when discussing 'disadvantages'), that the survey reports employers' perceptions, and should not necessarily be interpreted as indicating that particular disabilities in practice give rise to 'problems'.

Perceived 'advantages' of disabled employees

Of the 1,100 respondents answering the question, 29 per cent saw benefits or advantages associated with the employment of people with disabilities, and nearly half said they did not. Among organisations which employ people with disabilities, the proportion was higher, with 42 per cent seeing clear or explicit advantages in doing so. Respondents were asked to give brief details of the advantages they saw in employing people with disabilities, and these tended to fall into two broad areas: one primarily concerned with the motivation and dedication of the individual disabled employee; and the other with the enhanced image of the organisation to both other employees and customers.

Perceived 'disadvantages' of disabled employees

Among the more 'negative' aspects of employer perceptions, the most commonly reported reservation, cited by 56 per cent of respondents, concerned (potential) disabled employees' ability to do the job and their level of productivity. Extra costs were rarely seen as a concern, with fewer than one per cent of these respondents reporting this as a reservation.

Difficulties experienced in employing disabled people

Moving from perception to actual experience of employing people with disabilities, only 17 per cent of the whole sample stated they had experienced some difficulties employing people with disabilities. Among those who *currently* employ people with disabilities, the proportion of those who had experienced problems rises to 26 per cent. This still leaves three quarters of all those who employed people with disabilities stating they have experienced no problems in doing so. Again there is a strong size effect, with the likelihood of having experienced problems increasing with organisational size.

Respondents who had experienced problems were asked to indicate the nature of the difficulty and the disability in question. The most commonly cited difficulties were related to inability to do the job and low productivity, cited by a quarter of those respondents reporting difficulties. Following this were attitude and temperament problems and mobility problems cited by around 15 per cent, and problems in making accommodations for the disabled employees, reported by 12 per cent. These problems were supported by comments in the questionnaires and made during case study interviews. The latter also provided examples of a range of other difficulties faced which were not mentioned in the survey. These varied a great deal and were frequently not caused by the actual disability itself, but stemmed from a wide range of sources including management attitudes, economic circumstances and the physical environment.

The most common disabilities with which difficulties arose were mobility problems, with two in five respondents citing these. This was followed by hearing, with one in eight respondents reporting this disability, and epilepsy, wheelchair use, and seeing, each cited by around one in ten respondents.

The analysis also examined which disabilities were seen as causing which types of problems. Employees with disabilities affecting mobility were often seen as a source of problems regarding movement around the premises, access to facilities and equipment, and in jobs involving intensive manual labour. Sensory impairment and mental handicap were seen as a disproportionate source of difficulty with regard to job ability and productivity, and were the sole disabilities identified as a cause of communication problems. Allergies and skin conditions were cited as causes of problems regarding safety and hazardous materials in the workplace, while epilepsy was seen as a cause of safety problems and of 'problems among other employees'.

Disabilities perceived as barriers to employment

Finally, respondents were asked if they felt there were specific disabilities which would *prevent* a person being employed in the organisation. More than half of the 1,081 respondents to this question replied that certain disabilities *would* be a barrier to employment.

The largest category of disability seen as a barrier to employment, cited by two thirds of respondents, is again the broad group of disabilities affecting mobility and dexterity. Following this are the two sensory disabilities, seeing problems (cited by just under a third of respondents), and hearing problems (cited by one in six respondents).

Most of the cited patterns between particular disabilities and the *perceived* barriers to employment are familiar ones. Thus, use of the telephone is seen as a barrier for those with hearing difficulties and speech impairments; whilst use of computers, VDUs and paperwork is often seen as preventing those with seeing difficulties being employed; the layout of premises was frequently cited as hindering employment opportunities for those with mobility problems.

Actions taken to employ people with disabilities (chapter 6)

Nearly a third of the respondents to the postal survey had undertaken specific actions as a result of employing people with disabilities, in order to make it feasible or safe for them to do their job, or to improve their comfort or productivity (62 per cent had not taken any such actions).

Incidence of action by size

Yet again it was size rather than sector which appeared to have the greatest influence on whether actions had been taken, with the proportions increasing strongly from a mere five per cent in the smallest size category, to over 90 per cent among organisations with 5,000 or more employees. This variation is to be expected, given that the likelihood of employing disabled people itself increases strongly with employment size.

Incidence of action taken among employers with disabled staff

More interesting is the fact that of those organisations which *currently* had disabled employees, around *half* had taken actions to employ them. This suggests that despite the many obstacles and costs which employers *without* disabled employees typically anticipated in the recruitment and employment of people with disabilities, as many as a half of the employers who *had* employed disabled people had managed to do so, without the need to undertake any specific accommodating actions.

Disability types leading to action by employers

Respondents who had undertaken specific actions were asked to indicate the disabilities for which this had occurred and the nature of the action taken. The largest single category of disabilities for which some kind of specific action had been taken is the broad group of disabilities affecting mobility or physical dexterity, accounting for three quarters of respondents who had undertaken specific actions. This was followed by both seeing and hearing difficulties, accounting for just under a quarter of those taking action.

It is striking from the data, that none of the other types of disability identified led to action by significant numbers of respondents. Even more striking, however, is the comparison between the incidence of action taken for different categories of disability with the incidence of those disabilities in the sample of employers. Employees with mobility–related disabilities had led to action in 52 per cent of the organisations who employed them. When we look at *all* other types of disability, the corresponding proportions do not approach this figure. These data do *not* suggest an enormous burden on employers for most types of disability. Even mobility–related disabilities, which tend to feature most strongly in the popular perception of disability, appear to require action by about only half of those employers who have such employees.

Types of action taken

Not surprisingly, the main types of actions taken were 'physical', involving the provision of special equipment, or the modification of premises. Three quarters of organisations taking actions undertook them for people with mobility and sensory problems. Nearly all the other 'actions' frequently encountered, however, were organisational, involving modifications in the way things were done in the organisation. Modifying premises was almost exclusively undertaken for people with mobility problems and wheelchair users, while around half of organisations providing special equipment and training did so for people with sensory impairments, and raising staff awareness was most commonly undertaken in the context of employees with epilepsy.

Actions considered but rejected

A further indication of how 'difficult' employers found it to help or accommodate disabled employees was obtained by asking all survey respondents whether they had recently considered but rejected any of the kinds of actions discussed in the previous section. Only 17 organisations said that they had considered and rejected such action. None of this suggests that respondents confronted with an apparent need for action to accommodate a disabled employee were generally unable or unwilling to make that accommodation.

Perception of extra costs associated with employing disabled staff

A key issue clearly concerns the question of how much extra, if any, it costs for an employer to employ people with disabilities. All respondents to the postal survey were asked, therefore, whether there were in fact or whether they thought there would be, any extra costs associated with recruiting or employing people with disabilities. Of the 1,077 who answered this question 43 per cent thought there would be extra costs, 24 per cent did not and 32 per cent did not know.

Cost limits set by employers when employing disabled staff

A further set of questions asked how much extra costs employers were prepared to incur. Only a minority of respondents answered this set of questions, suggesting that employers do not tend to think in terms of upper limits to their extra expenditure associated with disabled employees. Comments written by non–respondents on the questionnaire and information provided by case study respondents support this suggestion. Whilst the small number of respondents suggests caution, the survey data did confirm that insofar as there are limits to the extra acceptable costs, the limits increase with the salary of the employee concerned, but not in proportion to the increase in salary. Thus respondents would be prepared to pay between five per cent for a higher paid employee and ten per cent for a lower paid one of gross annual salary, in initial costs of accommodating an employee with a disability. As far as ongoing costs are concerned, the corresponding range is between four and seven per cent of gross salary costs per year.

Finally, respondents were asked whether they would be prepared to spend more if the person in question was an existing employee. Of the 901 respondents to this question, 39 per cent said they *would* be prepared to spend more, 14 per cent said they would not be, and 48 per cent did not know. The proportion prepared to spend more was higher among those currently employing people with disabilities than among those who did not. This is consistent with evidence from the case studies that the larger organisations who are more likely to have employees with disabilities are also more likely to have experienced an existing employee becoming disabled, and understand the greater pressure to 'do the right thing' which such cases generate.

Use of external help, support and advice (chapter 7)

This chapter examines the extent to which employers have used external assistance or support in relation to recruiting/employing people with disabilities, and their views on additional forms of help, support or advice they might require in this area.

Extent to which external assistance is sought

Less than a third of respondents had sought such external assistance. Given the long–standing existence of provision of such support and advice through the Employment Service and the voluntary sector, coupled with the perceived difficulties of many employers in employing people with disabilities and their failure to meet their legal obligations, it might be seen as surprising that so few seek external advice.

Variation with size of organisation

Although there are significant sectoral variations, it again appears that many of these differences are essentially picking up a size effect. There is a steadily increasing tendency with increasing employment size to use outside support. This is a pattern familiar from studies in other areas of business and employment practice, namely that organisations apparently most in need of such advice and whose management and organisational practices could most benefit from it (namely the smallest firms) are the ones least likely to be aware of its existence, least likely recognise a need for it and least likely to seek it out. It seems that the understanding that there is some obligation to employ disabled people, that there may also be considerable benefits to the firm in doing so, and that 'good practice' implies a positive and pro–active stance, may be a message that has not reached many small organisations. Marketing of existing support and provision to such smaller organisations is therefore important.

Main sources of external assistance

When looking at sources of assistance, the main Employment Department organisations effectively dominate the market with nearly 80 per cent of this group using Employment Service (ES) provision and nearly half using Jobcentres. By comparison the other sources were used infrequently.

The main form of assistance provided by all the sources was *advice and information* (in each case over 80 per cent of those seeking assistance got this). In nearly all the cases the source provided *practical or financial help* about half as often as it provided advice and information.

Although there is a tendency for the use of all support sources to increase with size, the increase is most consistent for the use of the ES. Thus although the ES has the greatest share of this 'market' for all size groups, its relative advantage is far greater in the larger size groups. TECs and Local Authorities, by contrast, appear to do relatively 'well' in the smaller size categories, and it would seem that whilst smaller organisations are ill–served by most of the existing sources, some of the 'generalist' agencies are relatively more successful in reaching these employer groups.

Requirements for additional assistance/support

Finally the survey attempted to gauge the extent and nature of unmet employer need and asked if there was any form of help or support they would find particularly helpful. Only a small minority (16 per cent) said that there was some additional assistance which they would find helpful. Again there was a significant relationship with size, the largest organisations being eight times more likely than the smallest to think that additional external advice or support would be helpful.

Respondents were asked to indicate what would be most useful in this area, and it is perhaps unsurprising that the largest single category of greater assistance required was financial, with over a third of those giving suggestions, recommending more government expenditure on grants to enable employers to recruit and retain people with disabilities (these included wage subsidies and aid for special equipment). Some suggestions related to changes in the operation or emphasis of existing services, whilst others essentially saw public bodies playing a more effective co-ordinating role. In this context it is interesting that some of the case study respondents argued strongly that a major problem for employers in wishing to recruit actively from people with disabilities is one of accessing the pool of inactive or unemployed disabled labour — they would wish to deal with the voluntary sector as a potential source of such supply but find it fragmented, ill co-ordinated and competitive. On the legislative front, it is interesting that only two respondents argued for abolition of the three per cent quota whilst seven per cent argued for the introduction of anti-discrimination legislation.

1. Introduction

1.1 Background and objectives of study

The main rationale of the study reported here is to assess the extent to which employers are prepared to identify and meet the employment needs of disabled recruits and employees. In particular it aims to improve understanding of what employers are doing and are prepared to do with regard to recruiting and employing people with disabilities, and the areas in which employers are *not* prepared to act. It also aims to discover what kinds of help and assistance employers need if they are to do more in this area.

The study therefore examines what action employers who recruit and employ people with disabilities already undertake, why they undertake it, and at what cost. The study attempts to assess the actions and attitudes of employers in each of these areas with regard to a *range* of specific disabilities, as well as examining the benefits employers perceive in the recruitment and employment of people with disabilities.

The study also examines employers who do not employ people with disabilities, to discover why they do not, what obstacles they perceive, and what they might be prepared to do and under what circumstances.

Finally, the study aims to establish the kinds of assistance and support (financial and otherwise) which employers might find helpful in the recruitment and employment of people with disabilities (again this covers both employers who do, and employers who do not, currently employ people with disabilities).

1.2 Study methodology

To meet these objectives, a three–stage methodology was agreed with the Employment Department, the second and third stages of which were conditional on the outcome from the first stage.

1   **A literature survey** to establish what was already known on the above questions and the extent to which this knowledge can inform the current research.

2   **A postal survey** of employers to establish in broad quantitative terms, the current extent of recruitment and employment of disabled workers, and a picture of the distribution of attitudes towards disabled recruits/employees by type of employer.

3   A series of **in–depth** case studies of a sample of respondents to the postal survey, to obtain more detailed qualitative insights into the findings of the postal survey, and to pursue in greater detail employers' responses to actual and hypothetical examples of the recruitment and employment of disabled workers.

1.3 Literature survey

The first stage, the literature survey, was completed in January 1993 and presented in the form of an interim report to the Employment Department. This literature survey is included as Appendix 3 to the present report, and in broad terms it showed that while there is a considerable range of existing research on disability and employment, there is little up–to–date evidence on employers' practice and attitudes, and what there is does not go beyond the case study level at best, and at worst is anecdotal. The overall judgement on the basis of the literature/data review, therefore, was that there remained a strong case for the primary empirical research being undertaken.

1.4 Postal survey

The second stage of the study was a postal survey, in the field between January and March 1993, aiming at an achieved sample of around 1,000 respondents.

The sample had two component sub–samples (both drawn at organisation rather than establishment level) — the first was a random sample, which aimed at broad representativeness and was structured by employment size and sector. (SIC 0 Agriculture, Forestry and Fishing not included — see Appendix 1, Section 1.2.) The second, smaller sample, was a control sample of firms/employers known or believed to recruit/employ people with disabilities, and to exhibit 'good practice' in this area (*eg* they were users of the Employment Service (ES) disability symbol, or had received 'Fit for Work' awards in the past).

Full details of sample size and composition are summarised in Appendix 1, but in broad terms the total sample of 2,156 employers was made up of 1,855 employers in the random sub–sample, and 301 in the 'good practice' sub–sample. The overall response rate was 52 per cent (50 per cent in the random sub–sample, and 66 per cent in the good practice sub–sample). This overall response rate is a relatively high one for a postal survey of this nature.

There was no evidence of major response bias by size or sector in the random sub–sample (see Appendix 1 for discussion), but response bias could not be examined for the 'good practice' sub–sample, since overall sample characteristics were not available.

The questionnaire for the postal survey was agreed in discussion with the Employment Department and is included as Appendix 2.

1.5 Case study interviews

A selection of respondents to the postal survey were chosen for detailed face–to–face interview on the basis both of their structural characteristics and their responses to the survey — to cover those employing/not employing disabled people; those with 'positive'/'negative' attitudes *etc.* as well as sectoral, size *etc.* spread. The object of the case studies, which were conducted in March and April 1993, was to provide detailed qualitative insights to support the quantitative overview provided by the postal survey. The case study interviews involved a mixture of face–to–face and telephone interviews, in some cases with more than one respondent in a given organisation, using a semi–structured discussion guide, the content of which was agreed with the Employment Department. The total number of case studies conducted was 21, and again their main characteristics are summarised in Appendix 1.

1.6 Structure of the report

The report is structured around a number of key issues which were examined in the research, and the survey and case study results are integrated in the sense that we address each issue with both survey and case study evidence as appropriate, rather than summarising the survey and case study findings in separate parts of the report.

Chapter 2 looks in broad terms at whether or not employers have employees with disabilities, and how this varies by size and sector, the extent to which employees with disabilities were registered as disabled, and the main types of disability which were found in the organisations in question.

Chapter 3 singles out organisations who do not employ people with disabilities, looking at the reasons for this, as well as any perceived problems or difficulties associated with the recruitment, employment or retention of people with disabilities.

In Chapter 4 we examine whether or not organisations have policies on the recruitment and employment of people with disabilities, and the nature of the policies, with particular emphasis on the approach taken towards recruiting people with disabilities.

Chapter 5 considers problems or difficulties organisations have actually experienced in the recruitment and employment of people with disabilities, as well as any benefits or advantages they see or have experienced in recruiting/employing such people.

In Chapter 6, specific actions which employers have taken in order to recruit/employ/retain people with disabilities are examined, together with the costs of such actions.

Finally, in Chapter 7 we examine the extent to which employers have used external assistance or support in regard to recruiting/employing people with disabilities, and their views on additional forms of help, support or advice they might require in this area.

2. The Employment of People with Disabilities

2.1 Introduction

In this chapter, we look at the extent to which organisations employ people with disabilities. We look in turn at the incidence of employers with disabled employees, the characteristics of organisations who employ disabled people, the numbers of disabled workers these organisations employ, and the types of specific disabilities involved.

2.2 The employment of people with disabilities: employer incidence

Our survey asked whether the organisation or establishment currently employed anyone with a disability, whether they were registered or not. Well over half our respondents, 633 organisations representing 57 per cent of the total returns, replied that they did employ people with disabilities, while 42 per cent did not employ anyone with a disability, and two per cent replied that they did not know. There were considerable differences in responses between the random sub–sample and the 'good practice' sub–sample, with 92 per cent of 'good practice' organisations employing people with disabilities compared with only 49 per cent of organisations in the random sub–sample having employees with disabilities. However these figures may slightly underestimate the proportion of employers with disabled workers, as during our case studies we found that some organisations who had answered no to this question did, on closer questioning, turn out to employ some disabled workers who were not registered disabled, but who would strictly meet the definition used in the questionnaire.

2.2.1 Incidence by size and sector

It is likely that the characteristics of the employer will influence whether or not they employ people with disabilities. Table 2.1 shows the results broken down by the industrial sector of the organisation, and by its size, as measured by the number of employees, for the total sample, and Tables 2.1a and 2.1b (appended at the end of this chapter) show the results for the random sub–sample and the 'good practice' sub–sample respectively. The latter indicate, as expected, the much higher rates of employing people with disabilities in all parts of the 'good practice' sub–sample.

Looking first at variation by sector, for the sample as a whole, we can see that production organisations, and particularly those in energy and water supply, are much more likely than average to employ people with disabilities. Three quarters of organisations in the metals and minerals sector, and almost nine out of ten energy and water supply organisations employ disabled workers. By contrast, 44 per cent of construction sector organisations, and only 40 per cent of those in transport and communication employ people with disabilities.

Turning our attention to variation by size of the organisation, we find a clear pattern emerging. The likelihood of employing disabled workers increases consistently with size, so that although only 15 per cent of organisations with ten employees or less employ people with disabilities, all organisations with over 5,000 employees have disabled workers.

Table 2.1 Employment of people with disabilities by size and sector

	% Yes	No	Don't know	N=
Total	**56.7**	**41.5**	**1.8**	**1,116**
Sector				
Energy/Water supply	88.9	11.1	0.0	27
Metals/Minerals	74.4	25.6	0.0	78
Engineering	64.9	32.7	2.4	211
Other Manufacturing	70.8	27.8	1.4	72
Construction	43.8	56.2	0.0	73
Distribution/Hotels	52.8	45.0	2.2	180
Transport/Communication	40.4	55.3	4.4	114
Financial and Business Services	53.7	44.8	1.5	201
Other Services	51.3	48.1	0.6	160
Number of employees				
1–10	14.7	83.4	1.9	211
11–49	30.4	66.7	2.9	207
50–199	59.0	40.5	0.5	222
200–499	76.5	20.9	2.7	187
500–4999	95.6	3.1	1.3	159
5000+	100.0	0.0	0.0	92

Population of Table (n) is all respondents in sample

Note: Sector SIC 0 Agriculture, Forestry and Fishing was not included – see Appendix 1, Section 1.2

Source: IMS Survey

These simple bivariate analyses, however, cannot explain how much of this variation is due to the industrial activities of the organisation, and how much is due simply to size. The breakdown of employment size by sector, presented in Table 1.7 in Appendix 1, shows that SIC 1 (Energy and Water Supply) has by far the greatest concentration of large organisations, while the transport and communication, and construction sectors are dominated by small organisations. Therefore the high propensity to employ disabled workers in energy and water supply, as well as the low propensity in transport and communication, may simply be a reflection of the size distribution of organisations within these sectors.

2.2.2 Multivariate analysis

To draw out the individual influence of these two factors we need to use a multivariate approach. The strategy adopted is to undertake a logistic regression, or 'logit', analysis. This allows us to model statistically the probability (strictly the 'odds') of an event occurring. In this case the 'event' in question is the organisation employing people with disabilities. We can then define a reference organisation with certain characteristics, and look at the effect of changing one of these characteristics, but holding all the others constant, on the *odds* of that organisation employing disabled workers. Odds are simply another way of expressing probabilities, so if the probability of an organisation employing a disabled person is ten per cent, the odds are nine to one against, or 0.11.

The characteristics of the organisation we shall use in the analysis are the industrial sector and employment size used above, and in addition the ownership of the organisation (whether it is in the private, public or voluntary sector), and whether or not the organisation has a policy regarding the employment of people with disabilities[2]. We define the reference organisation as a private sector firm in the construction sector, employing between one and ten employees and without a policy on disabled workers. The coefficient for each variable is set to 1.0 for this category, and the coefficients for other values of the variable are interpreted relative to this reference category. Thus, a coefficient greater than 1.0 implies higher odds of employing disabled people than the reference organisation; whilst a coefficient less than 1.0 means that the odds are reduced in comparison with the reference organisation. As well as the value of each coefficient, we need to look at its statistical significance, and we take a value of 0.05 or below as 'significant', in line with statistical convention.

The results of the logit analysis are presented in Table 2.2. They show that after controlling for size, the influence of the industrial sector on the likelihood of an organisation employing disabled people is not significant, *ie* there is very little difference in the behaviour of organisations between the different sectors. In fact, the coefficients of the sector variable suggest that compared to a construction firm of a given employment level, an organisation of the same size in the energy and water supply sector is less likely to employ disabled workers, while one in transport and communication is more likely to employ people with disabilities, the opposite of what we found in Table 2.1.

By far the most significant influence on whether or not an organisation employs disabled people is the employment size. Care must be taken in interpreting this finding, however. The most obvious

---

[2] For statistical reasons we have amalgamated the two largest size categories

interpretation might be that larger employers are more likely to have favourable attitudes and policies towards the employment of people with disabilities. This may well be true, but it cannot be strictly inferred from this kind of finding, which can tell us very little about the behavioural differences between different sized firms. Even if the recruitment policy of all organisations was completely random and based, for example, on picking names out of the telephone directory, an organisation with 10,000 employees has more chance of employing a member of any minority group (such as a person with a disability) than does an organisation with ten employees.

Table 2.2 also shows that organisations in the voluntary sector are more likely to employ people with disabilities than are those in the private and public sectors, and that organisations with a policy regarding the employment of disabled people are more likely to have disabled workers than those without such. Again, both of these findings are consistent with prior expectation, as both voluntary organisations (many of which exist in order to promote the interests of people with specific disabilities) and those with a policy are likely to be 'good practice' employers regarding people with disabilities.

2.3 Organisations employing people with disabilities

For the rest of the chapter we shall be looking only at those organisations which employ people with disabilities. As mentioned above, 633 organisations replied that they employed people with disabilities, and the size and sectoral breakdown of this group compared with that of all respondents is shown in Figure 2.1.

Figure 2.1 Characteristics of organisations who employ people with disabilities

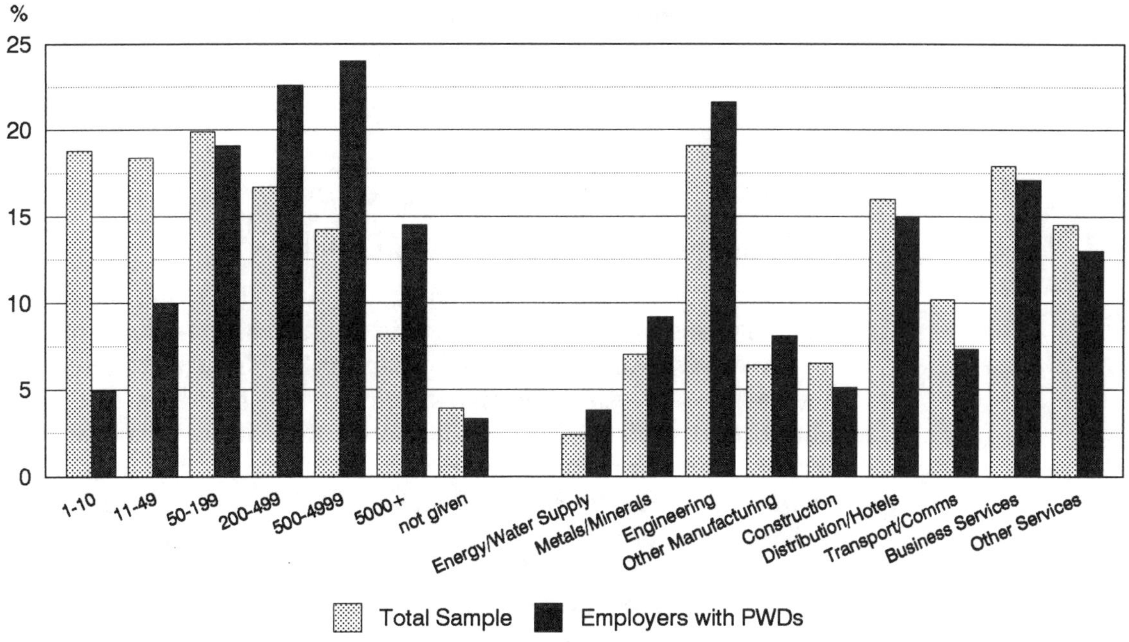

Source: IMS Survey

Table 2.2 Logit estimation of likelihood of employing people with disabilities

	Coefficient	Significance
Sector (construction)	(1.00)	—
Energy and Water Supply	0.87	0.87
Metals and Minerals	1.87	0.16
Engineering	1.57	0.19
Other Manufacturing	1.72	0.21
Distribution/Hotels	0.92	0.81
Transport/Communication	1.10	0.82
Financial/Business Services	0.79	0.52
Other Services	0.88	0.73
Size (1–10)	(1.00)	—
11–49	2.21	0.00*
50–199	5.56	0.00*
200–499	11.84	0.00*
500 and over	117.56	0.00*
Ownership (private sector)	(1.00)	—
Public sector	1.07	0.87
Voluntary sector	6.83	0.03*
Policy (no policy)	(1.00)	—
Unwritten policy	2.18	0.00*
Written policy	2.48	0.00*

*indicates statistical significance at conventional levels
Population of Table (n) is all respondents in sample
Note: Section SIC 0 Agriculture, Forestry and Fishing was not included — see Appendix 1, Section 1.2

Source: IMS Survey

2.3.1 Numbers of workers with disabilities

The average number of employees with disabilities among organisations who employ them is 22, and the average number of employees who are registered disabled is 20. However, these averages conceal the considerable distribution in the numbers of employees who are disabled. Table 2.3 shows that more than a third of organisations employ two workers with disabilities or fewer, and this proportion rises to one half when looking at workers who are registered disabled, although there is a considerable tail to the distribution, with more than four per cent of organisations employing 100 or more workers with disabilities.

Of course, the number of employees with disabilities within an organisation is related to the total employment level of the organisation. For a clearer picture of the levels of employees with disabilities within the organisation's workforce, therefore, we look at the percentage of total employees who are disabled.

Figures 2.2 and 2.3 show the frequency distributions for the percentage of total employees who are disabled and who are registered disabled respectively. Looking first at proportion of disabled employees, we find that employees with disabilities comprise less than three per cent of the workforce in 56 per cent of organisations, although the average proportion of employees with disabilities in our organisations is 4.5 per cent. This figure is slightly higher than the SCPR study[3], probably due to over-representation of 'good practice' employers in our sample.

Table 2.3 Numbers of employees with disabilities

No. of employees with disabilities	Percentage of employers with given number of employees with disabilities	
	Employees with disabilities	Registered disabled
2 or fewer	36.4	50.7
3–5	23.2	20.4
6–10	15.5	10.0
11–29	14.3	8.7
30–49	4.3	3.0
50–99	2.0	2.5
100 and over	4.3	4.7
N =	445	471

Population of Table (n) is all respondents employing people with disabilities

Source: IMS Survey

The distribution of proportion of employees who are registered disabled is skewed towards the bottom end of the scale, and shows registered disabled workers comprising less than three per cent of the workforce in almost nine out of ten organisations, with the average proportion being only 1.5 per cent. Although the Quota only applies to organisations with 20 or more employees, our results show that across all size bands it is only a small minority of organisations that employ three per cent or more registered disabled.

Both distributions have considerable tails but these are more to do with the arithmetic rather than the organisation being proactive in the recruitment and employment of people with disabilities, *ie* if an organisation employing four people has employees with disabilities, then the percentage of employees with disabilities must be at least 25 per cent.

---

[3]   Prescott-Clarke P, 1990, *Employment and Handicap,* London, Social and Community Planning Research.

Figure 2.2 Distribution of the proportion of employees who are disabled

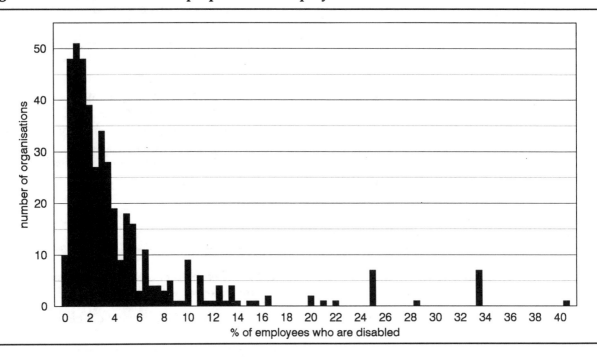

Figure 2.3 Distribution of the proportion of employees who are registered disabled

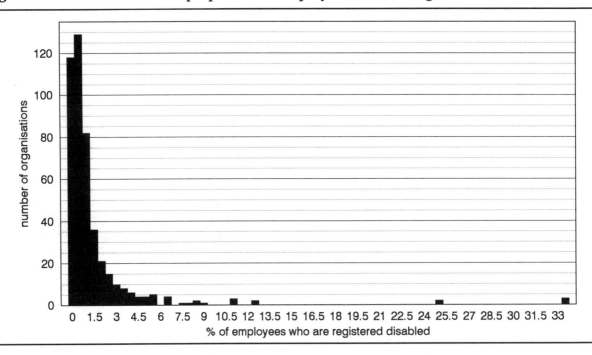

Table 2.4 shows that the proportion of total employees who are disabled in the workforce is 1.3 per cent, while the proportion of registered disabled workers is 0.6 per cent. Manufacturing industries have the highest proportion of employees with disabilities among their workforce, and the proportion of disabled employees in other manufacturing is over three per cent, while the lowest proportions are in the distribution, hotels and catering sector, and the financial and

Table 2.4 Percentage of workforce disabled by sector

Sector	% disabled	% registered disabled	% disabled who are registered
Total	**1.30**	**0.60**	**53.36**
Energy/Water Supply	1.27	0.73	67.41
Metals/Minerals	2.26	0.41	20.96
Engineering	2.45	0.98	46.41
Other Manufacturing	3.21	0.82	28.05
Construction	2.29	0.49	23.28
Distribution/Hotels	0.81	0.29	58.12
Transport/Communication	1.05	0.75	90.13
Financial/Business Services	1.01	0.47	43.12
Other Services	1.63	0.82	60.44
N =	445	471	374

Population of Table (n) is all respondents employing people with disabilities

Note: Sector SIC 0 Agriculture, Forestry and Fishing was not included — see Appendix 1, Section 1.2

Source: IMS Survey

business services sector. Looking at employees who are registered disabled as a proportion of total employment, we again find the highest percentage among two of the manufacturing sectors, engineering and other manufacturing, and also in the other services sector. Once more, the distribution sector has the lowest proportion of registered disabled employees amongst its workforce.

Finally, we look at the proportion of employees with disabilities who are registered disabled. Figure 2.4 shows that there is a large number of organisations which employ workers with disabilities but none of whom are registered disabled, and an even larger number of organisations which employ people with disabilities all of whom are registered disabled. Between these two extremes there is a reasonable spread, although it is rather more concentrated between 0 and 50 per cent, than between 50 and 100 per cent. There is also some sectoral variation, and as can be seen from Table 2.4, the average proportion of registered disabled employees among all employees with disabilities is 53 per cent, although among organisations in the transport and communication sector the proportion is 90 per cent, while in the construction and metals and minerals sectors the proportion is less than a quarter.

Figure 2.4 Distribution of the proportion of total disabled employees who are registered disabled

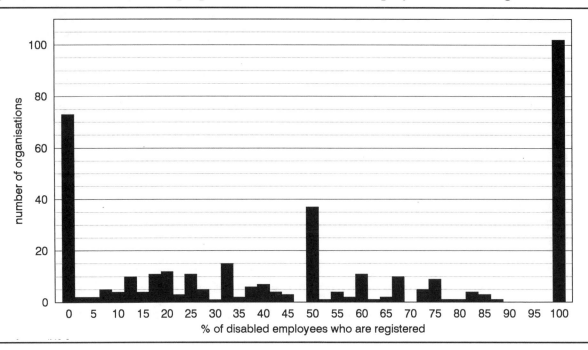

Source: IMS Survey

2.3.2 Types of disabilities

Respondents to the survey who employed people with disabilities were asked to indicate which types of disabilities they were aware of among their employees, from a list of fourteen broad types (see Appendix 2). More than one third of respondents replied that they had only one or two types of disabilities, while two organisations replied that they had more than 14 different types of disabilities among their workforce. The average number of types of disabilities was 4.5, and this varied from 7.7 in energy and water supply to 4.0 in distribution, hotels and catering and in the transport and communication sector, although again these sectoral variations are mainly due to varying size distributions of organisations within the different sectors.

The proportions of respondents citing each type of disability are shown in Figure 2.5. By far the most common type of disability is mobility problems, *ie* disability affecting mobility or dexterity of arms, legs, hands, feet, back, neck or head, including cerebral palsy, MS, and arthritis. More than three quarters of organisations replied that they had employees with this type of disability. The next most common types of disability are hearing problems, diabetes, and chest or breathing problems (including asthma and bronchitis), each cited by between 40 and 50 per cent of respondents. The least commonly reported disabilities were drug or alcohol dependency/addiction and blood disorders (leukaemia, haemophilia, anaemia), with fewer than one in eight respondents citing them. Just over four per cent of respondents said they had employees with 'other' types of disabilities,

Figure 2.5 Proportion of respondents citing each type of disability

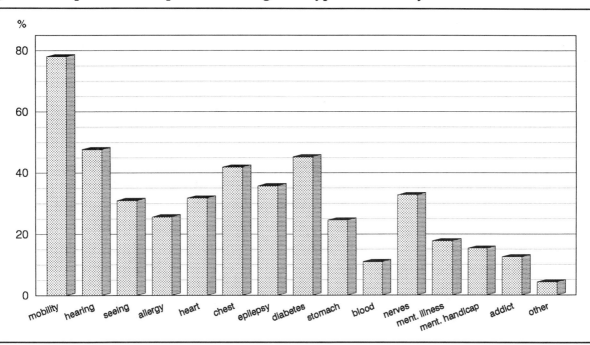

Source: IMS Survey

and the most commonly cited were speech impediments and cancer[4]. Table 2.5 shows the proportions of respondents citing each type of disability broken down by sector. The energy and water supply sector is more likely than any other sector[5] to have employees with each type of disability except mental handicap or other learning difficulties. All organisations in energy and water supply have employees with mobility problems, while the construction sector is least likely to employ people with mobility problems. The distribution, hotels and catering sector has the lowest proportion of organisations employing people with hearing problems, which may be due to workers in this sector needing to deal with the general public, and is also least likely to employ people with severe heart or blood pressure problems. The business services and other services sectors are more likely than average to employ people with sight problems, and these sectors along with transport and communication have high proportions of organisations employing people with mental illnesses or other nervous disorders. However, fewer than one in five transport and communication organisations employ people with epilepsy, which may be due to some of the restrictions in place regarding HGV and PSV licences.

---

4   This ranking of disability types is broadly in line with that revealed by studies of the incidence of disability within the working population (see the literature review in Appendix 3), although it should be remembered that the data in this Table show the proportion of employers who have employees with a particular disability, and does not indicate the overall incidence of disability within their workforces.

5   In the light of the earlier analysis, however, it seems likely that this is again related to the size structure of employment in this sector.

Looking at the manufacturing sectors, we see that the metals and minerals sector has the lowest proportion of organisations employing people with stomach and other digestion problems, and this sector, the engineering sector and the construction sector are less likely than average to employ people with blood disorders. The other manufacturing sector, along with financial and business services, is more likely than average to employ people with depression or bad nerves, and other manufacturing has the highest proportion of organisations employing people who are mentally handicapped. Finally, the construction sector is least likely to employ people with a drug or alcohol addiction, while almost half of energy and water supply organisations, almost four times the average, employ people with addictions.

Table 2.5 Incidence of different types of disability by sector

		% of employers in sector employing people with specified disability								
Disability	All	Energy/ Water	Metals/ Minerals	Engin– eering	Other Manuf.	Constr– uction	Distrib./ Hotels	Transport/ Comms.	Business Services	Other Services
All	56.7	88.9	74.4	64.9	70.8	43.8	52.8	40.4	53.7	51.3
Mobility	78.0	100.0	77.6	78.1	74.0	68.8	73.7	78.6	77.4	83.5
Hearing	47.6	87.0	43.1	51.8	48.0	50.0	35.8	40.5	51.9	43.0
Seeing	31.0	73.9	31.0	24.1	30.0	25.0	24.2	28.6	35.8	36.7
Allergy	25.7	43.5	22.4	19.0	30.0	28.1	28.4	26.2	29.2	22.8
Heart	31.8	52.2	41.4	38.7	36.0	31.3	18.9	33.3	30.2	21.5
Chest	41.8	65.2	36.2	44.5	44.0	43.8	36.8	42.9	43.4	35.4
Epilepsy	35.7	65.2	36.2	29.9	38.0	28.1	36.8	19.0	41.5	38.0
Diabetes	45.2	73.9	44.8	50.4	42.0	40.6	38.9	40.5	49.1	36.7
Stomach	24.6	47.8	13.8	24.8	20.0	25.0	18.9	31.0	30.2	24.1
Blood	10.9	30.4	5.2	7.3	12.0	6.3	11.6	11.9	14.2	11.4
Nerves	32.8	60.9	27.6	28.5	40.0	31.3	27.4	31.0	41.5	27.8
Ment. illness	17.7	34.8	19.0	8.0	18.0	12.5	13.7	26.2	23.6	22.8
Ment. handicap	15.3	13.0	17.2	12.4	24.0	12.5	17.9	14.3	10.4	19.0
Addiction	12.5	47.8	12.1	8.8	16.0	3.1	10.5	9.5	13.2	13.9
Other	4.3	4.3	5.2	4.4	2.0	3.1	3.2	2.4	6.6	5.1

Population of Table (n) is all respondents employing people with disabilities

Note: Sector SIC 0 Agriculture, Forestry and Fishing was not included — see Appendix 1, Section 1.2

Source: IMS Survey

Table 2.6 shows the patterns of types of disability broken down by employment size. For all types of disability the likelihood of the organisation employing someone with that disability tends to increase with the employment size of the organisation, although this relationship is not always clearly defined amongst the small organisations with fewer than 200 employees.

Table 2.6 Incidence of Different Types of Disability by Employment Size

| Disability | % of employers in size group employing people with specified disability | | | | | | |
	All	1–10	11–49	50–199	200–499	500–4999	5000+
All	56.7	14.7	30.4	59.0	76.5	95.6	100.0
Mobility	78.0	48.1	47.6	66.9	81.8	91.3	96.5
Hearing	47.6	22.6	14.3	30.0	46.2	59.1	90.6
Seeing	31.0	9.7	11.1	13.8	21.0	38.3	85.9
Allergy	25.7	0.0	7.9	16.2	26.6	30.9	50.6
Heart	31.8	3.2	12.7	19.2	29.4	40.3	63.5
Chest	41.8	19.4	17.5	20.0	39.9	55.7	80.0
Epilepsy	35.7	6.5	14.3	22.3	24.5	51.0	76.5
Diabetes	45.2	3.2	15.9	33.8	44.1	55.0	80.0
Stomach	24.6	6.5	12.7	11.5	22.4	28.2	55.3
Blood	10.9	0.0	3.2	2.3	5.6	14.1	36.5
Nerves	32.8	0.0	7.9	21.5	28.7	42.3	68.2
Ment. illness	17.7	3.2	4.8	7.7	14.0	22.1	45.9
Ment. handicap	15.3	0.0	7.9	7.7	11.9	18.1	38.8
Addiction	12.5	0.0	4.8	0.8	7.7	16.8	41.2
Other	4.3	0.0	3.2	3.8	7.0	1.3	8.2

Population of Table (n) is all respondents employing people with disabilities

Source: IMS Survey

Again, these simple analyses cannot separate out the effects of sector and size, so we have undertaken additional logit analyses to examine to what extent the apparent sectoral differences are due simply to the size distribution of organisations within each sector. As before, the reference organisation is a private sector construction firm, with between one and ten employees and without a policy on disabled workers, and the event in question is the organisation employing someone with the particular type of disability.

The results for each disability (not presented here for reasons of space) show that size is again the dominant influence. There remain, nevertheless, some significant sectoral effects, although there is often no clear intuitive explanation for this sectoral variation. The main significant sectoral variations which remain in the multivariate analysis are listed below (in all cases relative to the construction sector):

● the distribution, hotels and catering sector and the other services sector are significantly less likely to people with both sight and heart problems;

● the other services sector is also less likely to employ someone with bad nerves or depression;

● the metals and minerals sector is less likely than the construction sector to employ people with stomach problems;

● the energy and water supply sector is ten times more likely to employ someone with a drug or alcohol addiction than is the construction sector.

The influences of ownership and whether or not the organisation has a policy regarding the employment of people with disabilities are also generally significant. In particular:

● they are both a significant influence on whether the organisation employs people with hearing, heart and nervous problems as well as mental illnesses and handicaps;

● being in the public sector increases the likelihood of employing workers with hearing and heart problems;

● being in the voluntary sector increases the likelihood of employing people with mental illnesses;

● being in either the public or the voluntary sector increases the odds of employing people with bad nerves or mental illnesses;

● having a policy (written or unwritten) increases the odds of having employees with hearing problems or bad nerves; while

● having a written policy regarding disabled employees increases the odds of employing people with mobility, seeing, heart and chest problems as well as people with diabetes, mental illnesses and mental handicaps.

Appendix to Chapter 2: Data for the two sub–samples

Table 2.1a Employment of people with disabilities by size and sector

Random sub–sample	%			
	Yes	No	Don't know	N=
Total	**49.1**	**49.0**	**2.0**	**917**
Sector				
Energy/Water Supply	76.9	23.1	0.0	13
Metals/Minerals	66.7	33.3	0.0	60
Engineering	63.5	33.9	2.6	192
Other Manufacturing	63.0	35.2	1.9	54
Construction	40.3	59.7	0.0	67
Distribution/Hotels	48.4	49.7	1.9	161
Transport/Communication	35.0	60.2	4.9	103
Financial and business services	41.4	56.6	2.0	152
Other Services	34.8	64.3	0.9	115
Number of employees				
1–10	14.4	83.7	1.9	209
11–49	28.9	68.0	3.0	197
50–199	54.8	44.7	0.5	188
200–499	76.5	20.6	2.9	170
500–4999	93.4	4.7	1.9	106
5000+	100.0	0.0	0.0	16

Population of Table (n) is all respondents in random sub–sample

Note: Sector SIC 0 Agriculture, Forestry and Fishing was not included — see Appendix 1, Section 1.2

Source: IMS Survey

Table 2.1b Employment of people with disabilities by size and sector

'Good practice' sub–sample	Yes	No	Don't know	N=
Total	**92.0**	**7.5**	**0.5**	**199**
Sector				
Energy/Water Supply	100.0	0.0	0.0	14
Metals/Minerals	100.0	0.0	0.0	18
Engineering	78.9	21.1	0.0	19
Other Manufacturing	94.4	5.6	0.0	18
Construction	83.3	16.7	0.0	6
Distribution/Hotels	89.5	5.3	5.3	19
Transport/Communication	90.9	9.1	0.0	11
Financial and business services	91.8	8.2	0.0	49
Other Services	93.3	6.7	0.0	45
Number of employees				
1–10	50.0	50.0	0.0	2
11–49	60.0	40.0	0.0	10
50–199	82.4	17.6	0.0	34
200–499	76.5	23.5	0.0	17
500–4999	100.0	0.0	0.0	53
5000+	100.0	0.0	0.0	76

Population of Table (n) is all respondents in good practice sub–sample

Note: Sector SIC 0 Agriculture, Forestry and Fishing was not included — see Appendix 1, Section 1.2

Source: IMS Survey

3. Organisations not Employing People with Disabilities

3.1 Background

As already indicated in Chapter 2, of the 1,123 organisations responding to the questionnaire, 464 or 42 per cent did not employ any people with disabilities, and a further 19 (1.7 per cent) did not know whether they did. The energy and water supply sector had the smallest proportion of companies not employing people with disabilities whilst construction and transport and communications the largest with just over one half of these organisations having no disabled employees. As already discussed, however, size seems to be a more important factor influencing whether or not organisations employ any people with disabilities. Thus nearly 40 per cent of companies in the 1 to 10 size had no disabled staff, the percentage then falling to nine per cent for the 200 to 499 band, 1.1 per cent for 500 to 4,999 and none for the 5,000+. This accounts for the very small number of companies in the energy and water sector not employing people with disabilities since the majority of these are large organisations (and *vice versa* in construction, transport and communications with their high concentrations of small firms).

3.2 Reasons given for not employing people with disabilities

All respondents to the survey who said they did not employ any people with disabilities were then asked why they thought this was. Of the 482 organisations which gave reasons, just over three quarters indicated that it was because no–one with a disability had applied for employment in the organisations, although in a number of cases respondents felt it was possible that some disabled people might have applied, but not identified themselves as such to the employers. The following comment, given in responding to the questionnaire by the human resources manager of an engineering company with 130 employees, illustrates this although it is difficult to assess whether this is really the case or just guesswork on the employer's part:

> 'During recruitment drives over the last two years, only one disabled person has knowingly applied for a vacancy with the company. People are reluctant to say they have a disability for fear of discrimination.'

The other main reason given was that the organisation had employed people with disabilities in the past but they had subsequently left. This accounted for nearly one fifth of respondents. Only seven per cent of respondents reported that some had applied but were not suitable, whilst a further four per cent said that some had applied but were not recruited due to their disability which was a barrier for the particular job, three per cent gave other reasons and 1.2 per cent said they did not know why.

This pattern of response is consistent with views put forward during the case–study interviews. Most of the organisations interviewed, whether they employed people with disabilities or not, complained that the major obstacle to their increasing the numbers of staff with disabilities was that very few applied to advertisements, wrote in on the off–chance or responded to notifications sent to Employment Service Disablement Resettlement Officers.

Many organisations were extremely frustrated at the lack of response to their efforts to employ people with disabilities. The commercial director of an electrical engineering company stated that:

> 'Our single biggest problem was actually getting people with disabilities to apply. We just don't see them. Unless you are going to positively make the effort you won't get them. At present I have not got the time. We have temporary posts come up to fill a rise in demand and we want someone in post in a week. We do not have the time to go looking for people.'

This is not uncommon:

> 'Five years ago we tried to recruit people with disabilities to meet the quota but it was so unsuccessful that we gave up.' (Financial services company)

> 'The main problems have been disappointing lack of applicants. Response to vacancies has been extremely poor. It is often a scramble to get jobs filled within the four weeks notice period.' (Research and development group)

Case Study 3.1 — Construction Company

One of the organisations visited during the case studies was a small construction company which, despite the enthusiasm of the managing director for helping people with disabilities, had no employees with disabilities. He felt that:

'the company was not representative of the sort of organisation that could employ people with disabilities. The majority of staff all have to work on building sites or visit sites in some capacity. If they are in the office they are not doing their job. Building sites are very dangerous and have strict health and safety requirements. It is essential to be fit. Even someone with diabetes would be a danger to himself and others if working at heights and experienced a problem. You could argue that they could do the office work which takes place on site but even this would present real problems for someone with restricted mobility because they work in temporary port–a–cabins with rough surfaces. You can't build a ramp to a port–a–cabin in the middle of a building site.'

Opportunities for people with disabilities are limited therefore to the main office. A small company such as this only has three office staff — one secretary, one telephonist and an accountant. These posts tend to be very stable with low staff turnover.

It should be pointed out that when these same case study organisations were asked if they kept a record of applications from people with disabilities to monitor the numbers they receive, very few actually did. Several companies did not ask if the applicant had a health problem limiting the work they could do, and of those that did, most felt that the majority of disabled applicants would probably not admit to it at the application stage. This being the case, it would appear difficult for organisations to be certain that they were not receiving applications from people with disabilities[6]. Even so, those organisations which had tried other forms of recruitment aimed specifically at people with disabilities, for example recruiting through the Jobcentre, were often disappointed at the lack of response.

3.3 Variation by sector

When responses are broken down by SIC, most sectors followed much the same pattern as outlined above (see Table 3.1 below). Percentages for energy and water, metals and minerals and other manufacturing should be treated with caution since the number of respondents in these sectors was rather small. For the other six sectors, construction, at 85 per cent had the largest proportion of respondents indicating lack of applications as a cause for not employing people with disabilities, followed by financial and business services at 82 per cent. It could be argued that in construction many people with disabilities would not apply since the industry is generally physically demanding with few purely office based occupations (*see quote from case study — Case 3.1*). This cannot be the case with financial and business services, however. The smallest proportion (65 per cent) was in metals and minerals, although this represents only 13 organisations out of 20 responding.

The second most commonly cited reason for not employing people with disabilities in every sector, was that they had employed people with disabilities in the past but they had subsequently left. The highest proportion of organisations citing this reason was in metals and minerals at 35 per cent, although this represents only seven organisations out of a total of 20 who gave a reason. The two sectors with the lowest proportions giving this reason were construction, and transport and communications. In the construction sector only five out of 41 companies (12 per cent) cited this as a reason for not employing people with disabilities, which again might be expected in an industry with relatively few opportunities for people with disabilities. In transport and communications only nine out or 67 organisations or nine per cent had employed people with disabilities who had since left. This is not surprising either, because the transport sector has more health restrictions for drivers of commercial or passenger vehicles than other sectors. In addition, many of the respondents in this sector are small organisations with over a third

---

6 Case study respondents, on detailed questioning, generally confirmed this lack of knowledge, but some argued equally that insofar as the organisation did not know whether any unsuccessful job applicants were disabled, this implied that people with disabilities were not being 'sifted out' at an early stage in the selection process.

Table 3.1 Reasons for not employing people with disabilities, by sector

Sector	Percentage of respondents in sector giving reason						
	None applied	Applied but not suitable	Disability was barrier	Had some but left	Don't know	Other	Total (N=)
Energy/Water Supply	100.0	0.0	0.0	0.0	0.0	0.0	3
Metal/Minerals	65.0	5.0	0.0	35.0	5.0	5.0	20
Engineering	78.4	12.2	2.7	20.3	0.0	5.4	74
Other Manufacturing	85.7	4.8	4.8	23.8	0.0	0.0	21
Construction	85.4	0.0	2.4	12.2	0.0	2.4	41
Distribution/Hotels	76.5	7.1	4.7	24.7	2.4	1.2	85
Transport/Communication	76.1	10.4	9.0	13.4	0.0	7.5	67
Financial/Business Services	82.8	5.4	2.2	19.4	1.1	2.2	93
Other Services	76.9	5.1	5.1	14.1	2.6	1.3	78
Total	78.8	6.8	4.1	18.9	1.2	3.1	482

Population for table (n) is all respondents not employing people with disabilities

Note: Sector SIC 0 Agriculture, Forestry and Fishing was not included — see Appendix 1, Section 1.2

Source: IMS Survey

falling into the 1 to 10 size category. They are again less likely to have a large number of office based occupations.

For those organisations which had received applications but found the applicant not suitable irrespective of their disability, engineering had the most respondents with nine out of 74 companies or 12 per cent, followed by transport and communications with ten per cent. For the other sectors the percentages were low with seven per cent in distribution/hotels and five per cent in financial and business services. Construction had no organisations citing unsuitable applicants as a reason for not employing people with disabilities. This may be that many people with disabilities are aware of the restrictions in the industry and so do not apply.

Very few organisations (only 20 out of 482), stated that they had not recruited a person with a disability because their disability was a barrier for a particular job. The sector with the largest proportion was transport and communications with six organisations out of 67 or nine per cent of the total number giving a reason. This may again reflect the difficulties faced by the transport sector in recruiting people with certain disabilities as drivers.

Fifteen organisations stated other reasons, spread fairly evenly across the sectors, with none in energy/water supply and other manufacturing. Very few organisation said they did not know why they did not employ people with disabilities with only six spread across metals and minerals, distribution and hotels, business and other services.

3.4 Variation by size of organisation

Lack of applicants was far more frequently stated as the reason for not employing people with disabilities in smaller organisations, than in the larger bands. Just under 90 per cent of organisations in the 1 to 10 size band, felt that lack of applications was the main cause. With increasing size this proportion drops to three quarters for the 11 to 49 and the 50 to 199 bands, down to 63 per cent for the 200 to 499 and 28 per cent for the 500 to 4,999 bands (percentages for the largest size band are somewhat misleading since only seven organisations of this size gave any reason for not employing people with disabilities). Once again, however, we must be careful not to attribute over–strong behavioural interpretations to these size variations. In fact, the case studies and the survey (see Chapter 4) did suggest that larger organisations are more likely to have a positive policy aimed at attracting applicants with disabilities. Even if this were not the case, however, small organisations would still be likely, other things being equal, to receive fewer applications from disabled people than larger ones, if only because they are likely to be recruiting less often, and in smaller numbers than their larger counterparts.

For most size bands the second most commonly cited reason for not employing people with disabilities is that they had employed such people in the past but these had subsequently left. In the 1 to 10 size band only six per cent of organisations reported this as a reason, possibly reflecting the lack of opportunities to recruit people with disabilities in the first place. In the 11 to 49 band this rises to 29 per cent and for the 50 to 199 band the proportion reaches 40 per cent of respondents of this size. This percentage then decreases with increasing size, perhaps suggesting that larger companies have more opportunities for retaining people with disabilities.

Turning to organisations who had received some applications which had not succeeded because the applicant was unsuitable despite their disability; the proportion of such organisations increases with size rising from 1.7 per cent in the smaller bands to 57 per cent in the largest. Actual numbers are, however, small across all bands. Much the same applies to the other three categories, with only 19 organisations finding disability a barrier to the job, 15 giving other reasons and six stating that they did not know.

3.5 Problems associated with employment of people with disabilities

Of particular interest, as far as employers who do not employ people with disabilities are concerned, are their perceptions of particular problems or difficulties associated with the employment of people

Table 3.2 Reasons for not employing people with disability by organisation size

Size (no. of employees)	Percentage of respondents in size group giving reason						
	None applied	Applied but not suitable	Disability was barrier	Had some but left	Don't know	Other	Total (N=)
1–10	88.9	1.7	1.7	6.1	0.6	5.0	180
11–49	75.0	7.6	4.2	18.8	1.4	3.5	144
50–199	75.8	7.7	5.5	39.6	0.0	0.0	91
200–499	63.6	18.2	9.1	27.3	4.5	2.3	44
500–4999	28.6	57.1	14.3	14.3	14.3	0.0	7
Total	78.8	7.1	4.1	18.7	1.3	3.2	466

Population for Table (n) is all respondents not employing people with disabilities

Source: IMS Survey

with disabilities. Respondents to the survey who did not employ people with disabilities were asked if, in their view, there were any such problems or difficulties, and if so, what they felt was the source of these difficulties. The majority (68 per cent) responded that they *did* associate particular problems or difficulties with the employment of people with disabilities, whilst 21 per cent did not, and a further 11 per cent did not know.

Interestingly, there was little variation in this propensity by employment size, and a rather greater variation by sector — with construction sector employers being most likely to associate employment of people with disabilities with particular difficulties/ problems (90 per cent said they would), and financial and business services and other manufacturing least likely to do so (fewer than 60 per cent in each case).

Respondents claiming to perceive such difficulties were asked to identify the main source of the problem — from a list of twelve broad types (see Appendix 2). A significant proportion of those perceiving difficulties (42 per cent) gave only one source of difficulty, with a further 43 per cent indicating two or three. The largest number of options given was ten out of a possible 12 by three organisations. The average number of types of difficulty cited all respondents was 2.2 and this varied very little by sector, from 1.0 in energy and water to 2.5 in other manufacturing and financial and business services.

The source of difficulty most frequently given was related to the *types of work* or jobs the organisation could offer to people with disabilities (Table 3.3). This option was cited by just over three quarters of respondents. Very often, particularly in organisations with a high proportion of manual occupations, this was linked to the 'physically demanding' nature of the work, or to health and safety issues. Thus

Institute of Manpower Studies

a small firm in the metals manufacturing sector added the following comment to the questionnaire:

'The nature of the work of the company would mean that no person with any real hearing or movement problem would be safe in this factory. To employ someone in the office would mean restructuring the office, adding running costs and other long term expenses which would be of a permanent nature.'

These types of reasons, as we will see below (section 3.6) are by no means confined to respondents in manufacturing, thus the manager of a nursing home for *disabled* geriatrics argued:

'Because of the physical nature of the work,it would be extremely difficult for us to employ disabled people.'

The next three most frequently cited issues were all related to the *organisation's premises* (the characteristics of the premises themselves; access to the premises; and the cost of alterations to premises — mentioned by 41 per cent, 29 per cent and 16 per cent of respondents respectively). All other sources of difficulties were relatively rarely cited (by 11 per cent or less of respondents).

Table 3.3 Perceived source of difficulty in employing people with disabilities

Source of difficulty	% of organisations citing difficulty
Types of job/work	77.2
Premises	40.7
Difficult access to premises	28.7
Cost of alterations to premises	15.7
Cost of special equipment	11.4
Difficult journey to work	10.2
Concern that disabled workers might have increased sick	10.2
Concern about productivity of workers with disabilities	9.6
Concern about additional supervision/management costs	8.3
Attitudes of customers	6.8
Attitudes of other staff/managers	2.5
Other factors	2.2
Total (N=)	325

Population for Table (n) is all respondents not employing people with disabilities

Source: IMS Survey

It is interesting to note, however, that further questioning of such employers during the case studies suggested that many of these perceived difficulties are associated with somewhat stereotypical views of the range of disabilities likely to be encountered in the population at large. Although small scale and qualitative in nature, the case studies show that when asked exactly what it was about their premises which would make them unsuitable for, or too costly to adjust for, a disabled employee, respondents typically responded along the lines 'well, for example, a person in a wheelchair would just not be able to cope with the structure and layout of our building ...'.

It should be recalled, furthermore, that we are considering in this chapter employers who did not employ people with disabilities (although some of them had in the past). More generally, the case studies suggested further that organisations, particularly larger organisations, who *had* themselves encountered a wide range of disabilities, had a much broader image of disabled people, and were much less likely to think of stereotypical examples in discussing such issues. This suggests, perhaps, the benefit of work experience type placements for disabled people being targeted particularly at organisations with little or no experience of employing such people.

3.6 Source of difficulty by sector and size

Table 3.4 below examines the extent to which perceived difficulties varied by sector[7]. For every sector except financial and business services, the overriding difficulty was given as the types of work their organisation could offer. Over 70 per cent of respondents in each sector ticked this option, the largest proportion being in construction at 86 per cent. As discussed above, the physically demanding work often involved in construction is likely to be seen as a barrier by many organisations when it comes to employing people with disabilities (a point confirmed in the relevant case studies). This source of difficulty was given by similarly high proportions of respondents in the engineering, transport and communications and other services sectors. In financial and business services on the other hand, only half of respondents said that type of work was a barrier to employing people with disabilities. This is consistent with expectation in a sector where the majority of occupations are based in offices and are sedentary.

Case Study 3.2 — Retail Distribution Company

A small distribution company found their premises very limiting on the numbers of people with disabilities they could employ. They operated from an old building with no lift and no wheelchair access. It was not possible to widen doorways due to the age of the building and the use of large timber beams in its construction. All the office functions were carried out on the first floor and the nature of the work was argued to preclude anyone with any severe mobility problems from warehouse jobs.

---

[7] Percentages for energy and water supply, metals and minerals and other manufacturing should again be treated with caution since the actual numbers of organisations in these groups is small.

Table 3.4 Sources of difficulty associated with employing people by sector

Source of difficulty	Percentage of employers in sector citing difficulty								
	Energy/ Water	Metals etc.	Engineer- ing	Other Manuf.	Constr- uction	Distrib./ Hotels	Transport/ Comm.	Business Services	Other
Premises	50.0	33.3	35.3	50.0	38.9	54.1	30.0	45.3	35.2
Cost of special equipment	0.0	20.0	11.8	25.0	11.1	4.9	7.5	17.0	11.1
Cost of alterations to premises	0.0	20.0	13.7	25.0	16.7	14.8	7.5	18.9	18.5
Types of job/work	100.0	73.3	84.3	75.0	86.1	78.7	82.5	52.8	83.3
Access to premises	0.0	26.7	17.6	33.3	38.9	19.7	17.5	39.6	40.7
Journey to work	0.0	6.7	7.8	0.0	11.1	8.2	5.0	22.6	9.3
Attitudes staff/managers	0.0	0.0	0.0	0.0	2.8	4.9	0.0	5.7	1.9
Attitudes customers	0.0	0.0	0.0	0.0	2.8	11.5	0.0	17.0	9.3
Productivity	0.0	0.0	13.7	16.7	2.8	13.1	2.5	9.4	13.0
Sickness	0.0	0.0	11.8	8.3	5.6	13.1	10.0	13.2	9.3
Supervision/ management cost	0.0	6.7	13.7	16.7	5.6	6.6	5.0	7.5	9.3
Other	0.0	0.0	3.9	0.0	2.8	1.6	0.0	3.8	1.9
Total (n=)	2	15	51	12	36	61	40	53	54

Population of Table (n) is all respondents not employing people with disabilities who answered the question

Sector SIC 0 Agriculture, Forestry and Fishing was not included — see Appendix 1, Section 1.2

Source: IMS Survey

Premises was regarded as a difficulty by between a third and a half of all respondents in each sector ranging from 30 per cent in transport and communications to 54 per cent in distribution and hotels. This high proportion in this sector possibly reflects the until recent lack of perceived need to provide facilities in warehouses (*case study number 3.2*), and the fact that many hotels are fairly old buildings (*see case study number 3.3*). Premises was also regarded as a barrier by 45 per cent of respondents in financial and business services. Many organisations in this sector work through a network of high street outlets (*case study number 3.4*). These are often old buildings which are difficult to alter and may also be listed. Planning permission would not be granted for any major alterations, especially for external changes. It is also difficult to build ramps for disabled people which will extend into the high street pavement (further questioning of such organisations in the case studies, however, suggested that often these

> **Case Study 3.3 — Hotel**
>
> This case study involved a large hotel with over 300 employees, which currently employed no employees with disabilities (although some had been employed in the past). The hotel itself is in an eighteenth century (listed) building, with many narrow corridors and steep stairways, especially in the 'staff only' areas. The hotel's human resources manager, despite an expressed 'positive attitude' towards employing people with disabilities, felt that the age and nature of the building would render it unsafe for many potential disabled employees; and that the alterations necessary would be beyond the scale of any financial support from the employment service. This was seen as a key constraint on the possible recruitment of people with disabilities (others being the nature of the work — physically demanding; or dangerous, eg in the kitchen; and the perceived attitudes of managers and customers — although it was felt that the latter would apply only to certain types of disability, and certain types of occupation — chambermaids and telephonists were seen as having the greatest potential here).

objections applied more to physical adaptations to the building necessary for *customer access*, and as far as *staff* with disabilities were concerned, there were in practice often other solutions — such as adaptations of side and rear entrances — which could be adopted if appropriate).

As well as the characteristics of the premises themselves, 29 per cent of all respondents reported that physical access to the premises would be a barrier to the employment of people with disabilities. Around 40 per cent of construction, financial and business, and other services organisations and a third of respondents in other manufacturing sector felt that this was a source of difficulty. The lowest proportion was in transport and communications with 18 per cent of organisations ticking this option.

> **Case Study 3.4 — Financial Services**
>
> 'The problem with physical alterations is that often buildings can not be changed partly because there is not the room in front of a high street bank to have a ramp jutting into the pavement, but also because many of our buildings belong to English Heritage or have planning constraints.'

The cost of alterations and cost of special equipment were more important to other manufacturing, and metals and minerals than to other sectors (cited by one quarter and a fifth of respondents respectively) although the number of organisations involved is small. The proportion of respondents was also fairly high in financial and business and other services at 18 per cent for the cost of alterations; the cost of special equipment was put at 17 per cent in financial and business services and 11 per cent in other services.

Journey to work and attitude of customers were seen as barriers to a significant degree only by respondents in the financial and business services sector. With regard to customer attitude, in a previous study a manager in the service sector felt that the sight of a disabled woman disturbed customers (*Barnes 1990*). In sectors with a great deal of customer contact jobs often require applicants to be 'generally of good appearance'. Perceived inability to fit in with these requirements would preclude an individual from employment, although it became clear from the case–studies that respondents for whom this was an issue often had a fairly limited range of disabilities in mind (severe physical impairment, or 'appearance problems'/'personal habits' associated with mental disabilities were, for example, mentioned here).

The personnel manager of a medium sized retailing organisation commented, in this context:

> 'There is a perceived problem with customers if someone is disabled; if badly disabled, how this may affect customers. My personal belief is that many people do not come across disabled people in their normal daily work; they therefore are not sure how to handle it when they do.'

The breakdown of responses by size of organisation (Table 3.5) reveals a fairly uniform pattern across the size bands, indicating that among organisations who do not employ people with disabilities, size may not be a strong influence on the types of problems an organisation perceives. This does not imply that attitudes towards employing people with disabilities, and the perceived problems generated do not, in general, vary with size — all the case study and survey evidence suggests that they do. Rather, one interpretation of the findings in Table 3.5, is that those medium and large–sized organisations who do *not* employ people with disabilities (a minority, as we have seen), tend to have attitudes and perceptions which are more typical of smaller firms (indeed this may be one reason why they do not employ people with disabilities).

In all size bands the largest proportion of respondents indicated the types of job/work on offer as the most important barrier to the recruitment of people with disabilities. Interestingly, however, work type seemed to be less of a perceived problem in the smallest size category (with only two thirds of respondents mentioning it, compared with over 80 per cent in the other size groups). Premises–related problems, by contrast (particularly access and cost of alterations) appeared to be relatively more important to the smallest organisations, as did a concern about the possible costs of special equipment for disabled people. A greater anxiety about such cost–related issues is, perhaps, to be expected among the smallest firms, although case study questioning of small firms with no disabled employees indicated that their perceptions were often exaggerated (and again based on stereotypical assumptions that a 'disability' implied a wheelchair, or expensive equipment), and were often coupled with an ignorance about sources of support and finance available in these areas (*eg* from the Employment Service).

Table 3.5 Sources of difficulty associated with employing people with disabilities by size

Source of difficulty	Percentage of employers in size band (no of employees) citing difficulty				
	1–10	11–49	50–199	200–499	500–4999
Premises	42.5	35.6	42.9	38.7	80.0
Cost of special equipment	10.4	13.5	11.4	9.7	20.0
Cost of alterations to premises	21.7	12.5	14.3	12.9	0.0
Types of job/work	67.0	83.7	80.0	80.6	100.0
Access to premises	36.8	26.9	27.1	16.1	20.0
Journey to work	9.4	10.6	14.3	6.5	0.0
Attitudes of staff/managers	2.8	0.0	2.9	3.2	0.0
Attitudes of customers	8.5	2.9	7.1	12.9	20.0
Productivity	12.3	6.7	10.0	9.7	0.0
Sickness	13.2	11.5	7.1	6.5	0.0
Supervision/ management cost	7.5	8.7	7.1	6.5	40.0
Other	1.9	1.9	4.3	0.0	0.0
Total (N=)	106	104	70	31	5

Population of Table (n) is all respondents not employing people with disabilities who answered this question

Source: IMS Survey

3.7 Problems retaining employees with disabilities

Respondents who did not currently employ any people with disabilities were also asked if they felt there were any particular problems or difficulties associated with the retention of employees who have become disabled, the interest here being to see whether attitudes towards recruiting people with disabilities were different from those which applied when the person in question was an existing employee. Of the 464 organisations not employing people with disabilities 121 (28 per cent) said that there would, in their view, be such problems, whilst 155 (36 per cent) answered 'no' and 164 (or 37 per cent) said that they did not know. The key point to note, then, is that even among organisations which did not employ people with disabilities, attitudes towards the retention of existing employees who become disabled are considerably more positive than those towards the employment of people with disabilities in general. As we saw above, over two thirds of respondents saw problems or difficulties associated with the latter, as against less than a third when considering the retention of an existing employee.

> **Case Sudy 3.5 — Financial Services**
>
> A senior manager in a large financial services organisation, with a branch structure argued that 'in general terms we would do an awful lot to keep someone on who became disabled during the course of employment' and cited the case of a member of staff who lost both feet and part of both legs in a car accident — at a time when she was in a Branch. She was off work for some time, and then came back in a wheel chair. Not all branches have full wheel chair access (and this is seen as a major difficulty, given the number of old branches, and listed buildings) but they transferred her into a head office department which did have access. She now has artificial limbs, and so was able to go back to a branch, but the limbs have been giving her back problems, and she is having to return to a wheelchair. As this looked relatively permanent, they were eventually able to transfer her to a branch with wheel chair access, and she is currently working two days a week on a half day basis, and gradually increasing her hours.
>
> 'Financial constraints do apply in such cases, but when finance rules something out, we try to find alternative solutions rather than give up. So in the case of a very expensive building alteration for which no grant was available, they would attempt to move somebody to a different building/department. There are no guidelines or clear views on how much "too expensive" is, — we decide on a case by case basis. Generally, however, staff and managers have very favourable views towards disabled people (especially if they become disabled in the course of employment), the perception seems to be "it could happen to anyone", and are prepared to go to considerable lengths to help find an appropriate solution.'

This more positive approach was almost universally confirmed in the case study interviews (both among organisations who did, and organisations who did not currently employ people with disabilities — see case study no. 3.5, for example). When questioned more closely, a mixture of reasons was given by most respondents, including:

● **economic reasons** related to ensuring a return on the organisation's previous investment in training the person in question (several respondents drew analogies here with their approach to adopting flexible working practices, career break schemes *etc.* to retain women employees during child–rearing years);

● **moral and social arguments**: these were expressed variously in terms of the 'sweat equity' the person had in the organisation ('if they have been loyal to us, we should be loyal to them'), and the likely commitment of colleagues, and the poor effect on their morale if nothing effective was done to retain the person in question ('what if it happened to me?').

For both sets of reasons then, it was clear that organisations were generally prepared to go to considerably greater lengths, and greater costs (see also Chapters 5 and 6) to accommodate existing employees who become disabled, than to accommodate disabled recruits. Even in such cases, however, organisations stressed that there were limits to the extent to which such accommodation would be made, depending on the severity and likely duration of the disability/health problem, and several of the case study respondents cited cases where (usually 'reluctantly'), they had retired such employees on medical grounds.

Returning to the postal survey, responses to this question did vary by sector, with construction having the most organisations answering 'yes' at 40 per cent and the lowest proportion (17.5 per cent) answering 'no'. Metals and minerals, engineering, other manufacturing and distribution and hotels all had higher than average proportions of organisations not foreseeing any difficulties retaining employees who become disabled, the highest proportion being in metals and minerals. Transport and communications, business and other services were most likely to answer 'don't know', the largest proportion being in other services at 48 per cent. There was little variation in responses to this question by size of organisation, however.

When asked to list the source of these difficulties, around half of the respondents gave reasons related to the type of work, followed by 15 per cent listing productivity and 12 per cent stating premises. A further five percent were concerned with health and safety issues such as possible increased sick leave, general safety, ability of individual to pass annual medical and obtaining an HGV or PSV licence. When broken down by SIC the actual number of respondents is very small for each sector and reason given. It would seem, however, that looking at organisations who cited 'types of job/work' as a source of difficulty for retention, it was a less common problem in financial and business and in the other services sectors, and was most commonly cited in the transport and communications sector. Again these findings are broadly consistent with the case studies, with large financial and business and other service organisations in particular, stressing that the wide range of office–based activities, and the scope for flexibility in terms of hours and location of work, gave them considerable opportunity to accommodate the needs of employees who become disabled.

In sum then, it would seem that the major barrier employers without disabled employees feel that they face in both employing and retaining people with disabilities is the type of work they can offer. This is however less important in the financial and business services sector and slightly less important to the smallest companies, which were relatively more concerned with premises–related issues. Premises (including access and cost of adjustments to premises) were the second most common area of difficulties among this group as a whole. Finally, employers saw fewer obstacles, and/or were prepared to do more to overcome them in the case of retaining existing employees who become disabled, than with regard to recruiting disabled people in general.

4. Policies on Recruitment and Employment

In this chapter we examine whether or not organisations have policies on the recruitment and employment of people with disabilities, and the nature of these policies. This is the first action suggested by the Code of Good Practice and should cover the recruitment, training, career development and promotion of people with disabilities and the retention of newly disabled employees. Although not applying to the public sector, it is also a requirement of the Companies Act 1985 for companies employing more than 250 people, that directors' reports should contain a statement describing what policy has been operated in the previous financial year towards people with disabilities.

4.1 Organisations with policies

Under half of the organisations responding to the survey actually had a policy for people with disabilities. Of those only one quarter had a written policy, and the remaining 19 per cent said it was unwritten. 584 organisations (52 per cent) said they had no policy, whilst 28 organisations did not know and 15 did not answer. This pattern is broadly consistent with the results of previous employer surveys (summarised in Appendix 3), such as the IFF survey which found that only 21 per cent of establishments had any formal written policy (it is not easy to compare the RRC survey, since this looked at organisations which not only had a policy, but also those for which introducing one had been considered or was planned).

As Table 4.1 shows, the proportion of organisations with a written policy was highest in the energy and water supply sector accounting for two thirds of respondents followed by metals and minerals at 42 per cent. Around a third of the organisations responding in other manufacturing, business and other services had written policies whilst transport and communications on the other hand had the smallest number at only 13 per cent. Unwritten policies were most common in the energy and water supply and engineering sectors, existing in approximately a quarter of those organisations. Having no policy at all was most prevalent for organisations in the transport and communications sector (72 per cent) and construction sector (67 per cent). On the other hand, only seven per cent of companies in the energy and water supply sector had no policy and only approximately a third in metals and minerals.

Yet again, however, it seems that much of the sectoral variation is a reflection of the size structure of different sectors (Table 4.2). In particular, size of organisation was a strong influence on whether a written policy had been introduced. Only ten per cent of companies

Table 4.1 Type of policy by SIC

Type of policy	Percentage of employers in sector with given policy type									
	Energy/ Water	Metals etc.	Engin- eering	Other Manuf.	Constr- uction	Distrib./ Hotels	Transport/ Comm.	Business Services	Other	Total %
Formal written	66.6	41.6	17.5	29.2	15.3	19.8	12.7	30.2	34.2	25.6
Unwritten	25.9	22.1	26.4	19.4	18.1	20.9	13.6	15.1	14.9	19.2
No policy	3.8	32.5	54.7	47.2	66.7	57.6	71.8	51.3	46.6	52.7
Don't know	7.4	3.9	1.4	4.2	0.0	1.7	1.8	3.5	4.3	2.5
Total (n=)	27	77	212	72	72	177	110	199	161	100.0

Population of Table (n) is all respondents in sample

Note: Sector SIC 0 Agriculture, Forestry and Fishing was not included — see Appendix 1, Section 1.2

Source: IMS Survey

in the smallest size band had a policy at all and only three per cent of these had written it down. This rose slightly for the 11 to 49 band. Organisations employing between 50 to 199 people reached nearly half with a policy and just under half of these had it formalised in writing. The 200 to 499 size band only had one quarter of organisations having a written policy, which seems low considering the legislative requirements which apply in this area to all companies over 250 employees, although 58 per cent did have a policy of sorts. Having said this, only half the organisations employing between 500 and 4,999 had a written policy when in theory it would be expected to be 100 per cent. A further 23 per cent said their policy was unwritten. Even in the largest size band of 5,000 or more employees there were still a few organisations without a policy. Eighty-eight per cent said they had a written policy, seven per cent said it was unwritten, four per cent did not and one organisation said they did not know.

This pattern was confirmed by the case studies where it was found that the organisations with a written policy were, in the main, those that employed large numbers of people. Those with unwritten policies all employed fewer than 500 workers.

Further analysis showed that organisations employing people with disabilities were more likely to have a policy than those who did not. Nearly two thirds of organisations employing people with disabilities had a policy of some sort and 39 per cent had the policy written down (the percentage without a policy was 35 with 1.8 per cent not knowing). It is of course, difficult to attribute causality to these patterns; so, for example, it is likely that having a policy, particularly one which adopts a pro–active stance on recruitment, will increase the likelihood of an organisation having employees with disabilities; but equally, it is possible that having recruited a disabled employee, or having an existing employee who has become disabled, may be a trigger for an organisation to develop a policy in this area.

Table 4.2 Type of policy by size band

Source of Difficulty – Type of Policy	Percentage of employers in size band (no. of employees) citing difficulty						
	1–10	11–49	50–199	200–499	500–4,999	5,000 +	Total
Formal written	2.9	6.9	21.8	25.4	50.6	87.9	25.8
Unwritten	6.7	13.4	27.7	32.4	23.4	6.6	19.2
No policy	86.1	78.2	49.1	38.4	24.1	4.4	52.5
Don't know	4.3	1.5	1.4	3.8	1.9	1.1	2.4
Total (n=)	209	202	220	185	158	91	100.0

Population of Table (n) is all respondents in sample

Source: IMS Survey

4.2 Content of policies introduced

In the survey questionnaire it was not possible to go into further detail regarding the scope of policies or the motivations for introducing them. This was however, followed up in some detail in the case studies, which we discuss in this and the following two sections.

A key point to note is that most case study organisations saw disability as an equal opportunities issue, and as such policies on the employment of people with disabilities tended to be integrated into more general equal opportunity policies. Only one organisation in the case studies had a policy which was specifically for employment of people with disabilities. All the others with written policies said that it was part of a general equal opportunities policy covering race, religion, sex, marital status, any disability or other non job–related consideration.

The one organisation with a separate policy indicated that although they had individually addressed the three main areas of equal opportunities, that is women, ethnic minorities and people with disabilities, it was actually a three pronged equal opportunities policy and in practice the three areas were closely linked. *'A new initiative in one area tends to result in similar thrusts in others.'* In addition, if monitoring exercises are to be undertaken, it would be far more effective to monitor all three at the same time.

All organisations with a policy, whether written or unwritten, said that it covered all aspects of employment, and not just recruitment. Most written policies included statements such as:

> '... are committed to promoting policies of equal opportunity in all areas of recruitment, employment, training and promotion irrespective of an individual's sex, marital status, disability, age, race, colour, nationality, ethnic or national origin. .... will apply

employment policies which are fair, equitable and consistent with the skills and abilities of its employees,' (extract from EO policy in a financial services organisation).

Organisations which did not have a formal, written policy sometimes argued that there was not the need since it was an inherent part of their culture. *'We do not have a written policy, it is completely informal. It is simply part of company philosophy. The people who work for you are the most important asset and whilst we can afford to do it, we should do our bit for equal opportunities.'* In some other cases, the unwritten policy or approach had been generated by one individual who had developed an interest in these issues for some personal reason.

4.3 Monitoring

Ensuring the implementation of the equal opportunities policy relies on some sort of monitoring processes to be undertaken. Monitoring processes tended to depend very much on the size of the organisation. Case study organisations employing fewer than 200 staff tended to adopt an *ad hoc* approach to implementation and monitoring: *'the company is small enough and we know what is going on'*. Generally, in organisations of this size a single personnel officer or manager tended be involved in all outside recruitment and internal staff changes, and this central focus was sometimes used to justify the informal procedures adopted.

Larger organisations with policies on the employment of people with disabilities generally found the monitoring issue far more difficult. Those employing between 200 and 500 seemed to differ in opinion. Some believed that even with 450 employees it was possible to still keep track of all staff. Others were not so sure and were using piecemeal monitoring systems.

Generally, the largest organisations interviewed had more formal methods of monitoring, although they also felt that problems existed. Monitoring usually involved asking questions on application forms as to whether the individual had any health problems or disability which could affect their work. These data were usually analysed by the personnel department to monitor numbers of applications, and in some cases relatively sophisticated procedures were adopted, comparing the proportion of disabled people at each of the three key stages of the recruitment process (application; shortlisting/ interviewing; and appointment). In the largest organisations this analysis was often done at departmental or unit/division level, and in some cases targets were set for the proportion of the workforce which should be disabled (in the organisation as a whole, or for sub–organisational units), and at least one organisation set separate targets for the overall disabled workforce, and the registered disabled workforce (many of these monitoring issues are well–illustrated in *case study number 4.1*).

Several of the case study interviewees, however, felt it might be the case that many individuals will not admit to having a disability on an application form for fear of being discriminated against, and so the statistics produced are likely to underestimate the numbers of

Case study 4.1 — Local Authority

This large local authority, which has had a formal policy on the employment of people with disabilities since 1988, collects basic monitoring information on an EO monitoring form which is issued to job applicants, and kept separate from the main application form. As far as disability is concerned, applicants are asked if they consider themselves to have a disability, and whether they are registered. It does not record the nature of the disability.

Existing staff were monitored through an internal audit conducted at the time of implementing the EO policy, asking people to give their race, gender and disability. As in recruitment, disability recording was dependent on self-identification, although guidance was given on the form as to what might be regarded as a disability – the intention being to widen the definition as much as possible and encourage people to identify themselves as disabled. Nevertheless, it was argued '...*even if a blind person or someone in a wheelchair doesn't wish to identify themselves as disabled, they won't be recorded as such in our statistics. This is part of the problem we face in meeting the quota and our internal targets.*' Apart from this one–off audit (a follow–up to which is being considered), supplemented by data from the recruitment process, there is no mechanism for recording existing employees who become disabled, although if the personnel department become aware of it (*eg* because it is physically obvious, or has absence implications), the person will be asked if he/she wishes to be reclassified (again, however, the reclassification will not take place unless the person agrees, irrespective of how serious the disability is).

Since 1990, the EO Corporate strategy has set medium and long–term targets for disability (registered and non–registered) as a percentage of the total workforce, and at a departmental level (similar targets are set for race and sex). The targets were intended to be 'realistic' and were set in consultation with local disability bodies, on the basis of the expected size of the local disabled working age population. They are, however, considerably more ambitious than the three percent quota, and the council now believes they are unlikely to be met (in part this has been because overall recruitment activity has been considerably reduced since the targets were set). The monitoring data feed into management information as part of the performance management process. Departments make monthly monitoring returns to the personnel department, and forward all applications received from disabled people; if they are not recruited the personnel department goes through the application carefully to check why, in liaison with the department (the onus is on the departmental manager to justify rejecting a disabled applicant).

disabled people in the recruitment process (some argued that a similar problem applies to data collected on the existing workforce). As a result, some organisations had removed questions regarding disability because they felt it put unfair pressure on applicants to categorise themselves in this way, but this then meant that they have no idea as to whether they are attracting applicants with disabilities. These organisations did, however, tend to ask for this information on a new employee form which has to be completed once an individual had been appointed for a job. Thus, details of all new recruits with disabilities are recorded.

A further difficulty indicated by some respondents who had a recruitment monitoring system, with the monitoring information being kept separate from the selection process (in line with standard equal opportunities 'good practice'), was that this effectively prevented them from operating a 'Guaranteed Interview Scheme' for disabled applicants (the latter also being promoted, *eg* in association with the Employment Service disability symbol, as a key aspect of 'good practice') — see also section 4.10 below.

Monitoring existing employees was also seen as a difficult area. One organisation was developing a system for a monitoring process for internal job applications and promotions whilst another was planning to set up a register of staff with disabilities who were not registered, particularly those who had become disabled during their working life. A third case study organisation was running a pilot to monitor all staff which if successful, they planned to carry out every three years.

Such a process was not always seen as a straightforward one (see also *case study number 4.1*). Thus one very large case study organisation's personnel department had no record of the number of non–registered disabled. One of the company's main current initiatives in the disability area is to establish a register of all disabled staff, but:

> 'this has been in the pipeline for a long time, and little has been achieved. It will involve a lot of work with the trade unions and occupational therapists. Although the trade unions are in favour of any measure that will help improve the position of the staff, staff themselves are reluctant to register themselves as they perceive it as some form of threat or as limiting their chances of career progression. We have to think of ways to overcome this.' (Transport and communications organisation).

One company simply felt that the issue was too sensitive and so were not planning to gather information on non–registered people with disabilities. *'This is a sensitive matter and people would be concerned about offering the information'.*

4.4 Implementation

Implementation of policies was seen as difficult by most personnel managers in the case study organisations. In smaller organisations they tended to rely, as with monitoring, on there being so few staff that they could personally keep track of what was going on. This applied to some organisations employing up to 500 staff. Others however, felt they only had a partial understanding of the situation. One personnel officer said that if she personally did all the interviewing she did know what was happening. Unfortunately this was being handed down to the supervisors for the manufacturing staff and she had some doubts as to how she was to be sure their policy was being implemented. It was also pointed out by one personnel manager that although she may be involved with all recruitment and selection externally, internal processes were less straightforward to monitor.

> 'It's all very well monitoring new recruits to jobs or internal transfers, the problem is what happens before that. There may be reasons for someone not applying for a job because they have already been blocked by their manager. This is very difficult to monitor,' (Business services organisation).

Another felt that although line managers were directly responsible for dealing with the disability issue and that they had all been given the appropriate equal opportunities training, she relied on the approach in the personnel office to be sufficiently friendly and informal that people with problems would come to them and advise them of any discriminatory practices taking place.

When organisations with policies on disability were too large for central personnel staff to be involved in all recruitment and selection, the majority made sure that all managers with recruitment responsibilities underwent training in selection techniques including equal opportunity and disability issues. At least one organisation had had to develop equal opportunity implementation procedures in their bid to obtain BS5750. This also involved training all management staff down to a supervisory level covering recruitment, disciplinary and equal opportunity issues. The personnel manager argued, nevertheless, that despite such training, effective implementation was heavily reliant on the individual manager's commitment.

In addition to 'top down' monitoring systems, targets and training programmes, some larger organisations stressed the need for a 'bottom up' element to reinforce the pressure for implementation. Typically, this involved informing individual staff of the organisation's equal opportunities policy (explicit and serious endorsement of the policy from the Chief Executive or similar was seen to be important for staff to take this seriously), and of the mechanisms for complaint. Most of such organisations had general guides to equal opportunities including disability. One organisation was producing a booklet which was aimed specifically at people with disabilities and their line managers.

Others had undertaken more imaginative actions to attempt to push the equal opportunities message. One organisation had employed the ES to do a research project for them involving talking to staff with disabilities, managers, colleagues and trainers to come up with key action points, one of which was awareness training for key personnel. The same organisation had also set up a small working group to look at disability issues, make recommendations on an ongoing basis and to put together examples of good practice.

In very large organisations uniformity of approach was seen as very hard to achieve throughout all divisions or units. In order to overcome this one company had regular monthly meetings between the Equal Opportunities Advisors and personnel specialists. The EO Advisors act as the main link between head office and the divisional managers.

Despite the numerous initiatives employed by the different case study organisations, in medium and large organisations, it was often felt that implementation is ultimately reliant on the approach of individual line managers at site or divisional level. Thus one respondent argued that whether a person with a disability got the right equipment or not *still depends on the support they get from their line manager and the personal relationship between the staff member and his/her manager.*' For such organisations, implementation of equal opportunity policy in general, and disability policy in particular, was often reduced to simple statements of faith:

> 'We rely a lot on simple communication and the hope that the type of people we employ as managers will have the same belief in equal opportunities.' (Wholesale distribution company).

4.5 Recruitment of people with disabilities

Returning to the survey, a set of questions was asked about policies and practices adopted in relation to the recruitment of people with disabilities. Organisations were asked whether they actively sought to recruit people with disabilities, what vacancies this policy applied to and by which methods they did so.

Table 4.3 Organisations actively seeking to recruit disabled by sector

Actively seeking to recruit disabled?	Percentage of employers in sector giving response									
	Energy/ Water	Metals etc.	Engin- eering	Other Manuf	Constr- uction	Distrib./ Hotels	Transp./ Comm.	Bus Services	Other	Total %
Yes	55.5	16.9	17.8	19.4	8.2	16.4	8.9	21.6	27.6	19.1
No	37.0	77.9	79.9	77.8	86.3	79.1	82.1	73.4	65.0	75.8
Don't know	7.4	5.2	2.3	2.8	5.5	4.5	8.9	5.0	7.4	5.1
Total (n=)	27	77	214	72	73	177	112	199	163	100.0

Population for Table (n) is all respondents in sample

Sector SIC 0 Agriculture, Forestry and Fishing was not included — see Appendix 1, Section 1.2

Source: IMS Survey

Of all the organisations responding to the survey, only one in five said they were actively seeking to recruit people with disabilities, three quarters answered 'no' and five per cent said they did not know. By sector (Table 4.3), the construction industry was least active in recruiting people with disabilities with only eight per cent of companies answering 'yes'. The most active in recruiting people with disabilities was the energy and water supply sector with just over half the organisations indicating that they were doing something although there were only 27 respondents in this sector. This was followed by business and other services with 22 per cent and 28 per cent respectively.

Once again, size seemed a strong influence on the existence of such recruitment policies, with the numbers of organisations actively recruiting people with disabilities very low in the 1 to 10 band at only 1.4 per cent, but rising to nearly two thirds among organisations employing over 5,000 employees.

Table 4.4 Organisations actively seeking to recruit disabled by size

Actively seeking to recruit disabled?	Percentage of employers in size band (no. of employees) citing difficulty						
	1–10	11–49	50–199	200–499	500–4,999	5,000+	Total %
Yes	1.4	4.4	15.8	23.0	36.1	65.9	19.3
No	91.4	90.2	79.3	72.7	60.8	30.8	75.7
Don't know	7.2	5.4	5.0	4.3	3.2	3.3	4.9
Total (n=)	209	205	222	187	158	91	100.0

Population of Table (n) is all respondents in sample

Source: IMS Survey

Whether organisations already employed people with disabilities was also an important factor. Of those that had disabled employees, 32 per cent said they were actively recruiting more. Even among this group, however, nearly two thirds were not. On the other hand among companies which had no employees with disabilities, only five per cent said they were actively seeking to recruit people with disabilities. Again, however, the causality underlying this relationship could operate in either direction (actively seeking disabled recruits results in getting some and/or having disabled employees leads to adoption of a recruitment policy).

Although this appears on the surface to be a rather depressing outlook for the recruitment of people with disabilities, in that few organisations are actually doing anything, this is not necessarily a reflection of apathy towards disability issues. Comments from both the questionnaires and case studies indicate that many organisations would be very keen to do more but at present due to the recession they simply are not employing any staff. This impression was very strong from smaller companies who responded to the questionnaire. The comments were fairly typical:

'In the current business climate it is perhaps too easy for employers to "select out" on cost grounds.' (Electronics company)

'In these difficult times it is not easy to fill in a questionnaire like this one. We are currently having to lay people off and don't like it!' (Textile engineering company)

'Please note that we have had little/no recruitment of any kind in recent years, and this trend is likely to continue.' (Automotive components company)

'The industry as a whole is in depression. Profits are difficult to attain, therefore it is not possible to increase outgoings to employ people with disabilities.' (Travel agent)

'Unemployment is so high and many companies are finding it difficult to keep going. Therefore disabled people are not being considered seriously.' (Engineering company)

Despite this, some employers expressed the opinion that it was counter productive to single out people with disabilities and that they should be treated like every one else.

'No employer should seek actively to employ disabled people as this serves simply to create often inferior conditions of work.' (Road haulage company)

Even the largest organisations said that the only recruitment they were undertaking was replacement of key specialist staff. Among the case studies, at least half specifically indicated that all recruitment was at a standstill. Only one case study organisation (employing over 500) did not specifically indicate that they were not recruiting at present, and two public sector organisations said that they were reducing staff numbers. Again comments such as the one below were common.

'Frankly our response is patchy and perhaps less than perfect in recession times.' (Financial services organisation)

'At present the problem is that we are doing very little external recruitment. Our staff numbers are actually going down.' (Manufacturing company)

4.6 Vacancies specified for people with disabilities

Those organisations which did actively seek to recruit people with disabilities, were asked whether this was for all vacancies, a specified range of vacancies or specific vacancies on a case-by–case basis. Of the 206 organisations which answered the question, nearly half indicated that they actively sought to recruit people with disabilities to all vacancies. Thirty seven per cent said that recruitment activity was for specified vacancies on a case by case basis and only 15 per cent said that a specified range applied.

Broken down by sector, Table 4.5 shows that the largest proportion of respondents answering that the approach applied to all vacancies was in the other services sector followed by energy and water supply — this is likely to reflect the influence of size, as well as the fact that many organisations in the other services sector are public or voluntary sector organisations which are more likely to have a strong and proactive recruitment strategy here. The smallest proportion was in construction with only one organisation taking such an approach.

Very few organisations with a proactive recruitment strategy limited recruiting people with disabilities to a specified range of vacancies, but of those the largest proportion was in distribution and hotels. Recruiting people with disabilities to specific vacancies on a case–by–case basis was most often used in the construction sector with two thirds of organisations operating this policy followed by distribution and hotels. The lowest proportion was in the other services sector at 16 per cent.

Table 4.5 Vacancies to which organisations recruit disabled by sector

Type of vacancy	Percentage of employers in sector recruiting in specified fashion									
	Energy/ water	Metals etc.	Engin- eering	Other Manuf.	Constr- uction	Distrib./ Hotels	Trans./ Comm.	Business Services	Other	Total %
All Vacancies	66.7	46.2	35.3	42.9	16.7	20.7	44.4	51.2	71.1	47.6
Specified Range	13.3	7.7	17.6	21.4	16.7	24.1	11.1	9.8	13.3	15.0
Specific Vacancies	20.0	46.2	47.1	35.7	66.7	55.2	44.4	39.0	15.6	37.4
Total	15	13	34	14	6	29	9	41	45	206

Population of Table (n) is all respondents who actively seek to recruit people with disabilities

Note: Sector SIC 0 Agriculture, Forestry and Fishing was not included — see Appendix 1, Section 1.2

Source: IMS Survey

The smallest size band had roughly one third of respondents attracting people with disabilities to all vacancies and two thirds to a specific vacancies on a case–by–case basis probably reflecting the very small amount of recruitment they are involved in. Organisations with between 11 to 49 employees on the other hand had more responding that recruitment efforts were for all vacancies with only a third employing on a case by case basis. The number of total responses for both groups was very small. The 50 to 199 group had responses fairly equally split between all options. The next three size bands follow the pattern that with increasing size, the numbers recruiting for all vacancies increases, whilst working on a case by case bases declines.

The case study organisations included examples of all three approaches. Those which said they opened all vacancies to people with disabilities generally relied either on the use of an equal opportunities statement on their advertising material and/or the notification of all vacancies to the DRO.

Several case study organisations indicated that they prioritised a range of vacancies specifically for people with disabilities. One approach here (unusual in that the range of vacancies prioritised were at a relatively high level in the occupational hierarchy) was found in

Table 4.6 Vacancies to which organisations recruit disabled by size band

Type of Vacancy	Percentage of employers in size band (no. of employees) recruiting in specified fashion						
	1–10	11–49	50–199	200–499	500– 4,999	5,000+	Total %
All Vacancies	33.3	55.6	37.1	40.5	49.1	59.3	48.3
Specified Range	0.0	11.1	31.4	9.5	13.2	10.2	14.4
Specific Vacancies	66.7	33.3	31.4	50.0	37.7	30.5	37.3
Total	3	9	35	42	53	59	201

Population of Table (n) is all respondents who actively seek to recruit people with disabilities

Source: IMS Survey

an organisation which decided specifically to target students with disabilities at some of their graduate milkround tours. To facilitate this a member of staff had been trained in sign language.

Other organisations argued that only certain jobs would be suitable for people with disabilities, because of restrictions relating to occupations which dominated their workforce. Thus one organisation which provided laboratory services to the consumer product industry offered only administrative jobs to people with disabilities because there were numerous health and safety restrictions regarding employment of laboratory staff. Similar comments were made on questionnaires by organisations in the transport sector regarding HGV and PSV drivers, and in the construction sector regarding site workers.

Some occupations in a case study electrical engineering company were specifically set aside for people with disabilities. A sub–assembly part of the factory had deliberately not been mechanised in order to keep open jobs for staff with disabilities.

Two case study organisations set aside specific temporary posts for people with disabilities, who were prioritised in the selection process. Both organisations were recruiting very few permanent staff and saw this as an opportunity for people with disabilities to get at least some experience within the company, prove their abilities and enhance their chances of getting a permanent job should a vacancy subsequently arise (see *case study number 4.2*).

In two of the case studies the personnel managers said they reviewed each vacancy on a case–by–case basis. In both cases this was done using the help of the Employment Service disability adviser to identify suitable vacancies for people with disabilities (*case study number 4.3*).

4.7 Attracting job applicants with disabilities

The next part of the questionnaire aimed to get further detail as to how organisations who were actively seeking to recruit people with disabilities, went about attracting job applicants with disabilities. Respondents were asked to indicate whether they sent specific requests to Jobcentres and Careers Offices, whether they used job advertisements welcoming disabled applicants, if they notified the DRO or DEA, whether they contacted voluntary organisations or used other methods.

The two most frequently used methods were job advertisements welcoming disabled applicants and notifying the DRO or DEA, both of which were used by approximately half of these respondents. This was followed by 43 per cent of organisations who also said they used Jobcentres and Careers Offices.

Table 4.7 shows that specifically–worded advertisements was most commonly used in the other services and energy and water supply sectors followed by transport and communications. Sending all job adverts to the DRO or DEA was also most frequently used by other services. All sectors except distribution and hotels and financial and business services had over half of respondents indicating that this was one method of recruitment they used.

Case Study 4.3 — Computer Based Training Company

This is a small but expanding company whose managing director decided that they should employ a person with a disability. They reviewed the current vacancies and although there was a post for an office junior, they felt this would involve to much 'go–for' work and would exclude a person with mobility problems. Once a suitable vacancy as an accounts clerk came up, they consulted the local Disablement Rehabilitation Officer to ensure that it would be possible for a person with a disability to do the work and to put forward some suitable candidates. At the same time an occupational therapist came to the office to see what structural changes would be necessary to employ someone using a wheelchair. The woman they eventually employed, although not in a wheelchair, had severe mobility problems. The company was extremely happy with her progress — 'she is a real find'.

Table 4.7 Method of attracting people with disabilities by sector

Method	Percentage of employers in sector using method									
	Energy/ Water	Metals etc.	Engin- eering	Other Manuf.	Constr- uction	Dist./ Hotels	Trans./ Comm	Business Services	Other	Total %
Job/Centre Careers Office	33.3	61.5	45.9	57.1	16.7	55.6	50.0	34.1	35.6	42.8
Job Advert Welcoming Disabled	73.3	38.5	35.1	35.7	50.0	33.3	60.0	48.8	75.6	51.0
Notify DRO/DEA	53.3	53.8	54.1	64.3	50.0	40.7	50.0	39.0	68.9	52.9
Notify Voluntary Organisation	40.0	0.0	2.7	14.3	33.3	14.8	10.0	19.5	24.4	16.8
Other Method(s)	0.0	7.7	2.7	0.0	0.0	11.1	10.0	4.9	11.1	6.3
Total	15	13	37	14	6	27	10	41	45	208

Population of Table (n) is all respondents who actively seek to recruit people with disabilities

Note: Sector SIC 0 Agriculture, Forestry and Fishing was not included — see Appendix 1, Section 1.2

Source: IMS Survey

Table 4.8 Method of attracting applicants with disabilities, by size

Method	Percentage of employers in size band (no. of employees) using method						
	1 – 10	11 – 49	50 – 199	200 – 499	500 – 4999	5000+	Total %
Job Centre/ Careers Office	0.0	55.6	48.6	45.2	40.7	37.3	42.1
Job Advert Welcoming Disabled	0.0	33.3	45.7	28.6	64.8	66.1	52.0
Notify DRO/DEA	33.3	33.3	42.9	61.9	51.9	61.0	54.0
Notifying Voluntary Organisation	0.0	11.1	2.9	4.8	27.8	27.1	17.3
Other Method(s)	0.0	11.1	0.0	7.1	3.7	11.9	6.4
Total	3	9	35	42	54	59	202

Population of Table (n) is all respondents who actively seek to recruit people with disabilities

Source: IMS Survey

Case Study 4.4 — Local Authority

People with disabilities were actively sought for all vacancies. All advertisements carry the EO policy details and all say that disabled applicants who meet the job specification (no proof is required) will be guaranteed an interview. All vacancies are posted in a fortnightly bulletin, posted in all council buildings (so the public can also see it), and is sent to a long list of local organisations active in the disability field (as well as women's and ethnic and community groups). It automatically goes to DROs/PACT members, and the Jobcentres. All job advertisements and the vacancies bulletin can be made available in alternative forms (tape, braille *etc.*).

The guaranteed interview scheme may be strengthened in the near future to guarantee appointment to disabled candidates who meet the job criteria. The council is considering setting up an employment register of disabled people seeking work, to whom the vacancy bulletin will be sent; the register will be set up through press advertising and community groups (no proof of disability will be required to go onto the register).

A lot of detailed monitoring of the recruitment and selection process is undertaken, looking at the proportion of applicants who are disabled, and the proportions who get shortlisted and selected. The key problem for improving the representation of disabled people is the low proportion at the first (application) stage. A major current question is 'whether there really are as many disabled people out there looking for jobs as the voluntary groups argue, or whether it's just (despite our efforts) they don't regard the council as an attractive place to work'.

Compulsory Competitive Tendering (CCT) is causing many difficulties in implementing recruitment policies (affecting all areas of EO, including disability). Some managers are now pushing for simultaneous advertising, rather than going through the vacancy bulletin first, and some have attempted to bypass the prescribed procedures altogether (eg. bringing forward closing dates for applications *etc.*).

All vacancies must be put before a 'monitoring sub-committee' which looks at the relevance of the qualifications for the job in question; and takes them out if they are not. As part of general EO practice they are gradually moving away from the use of qualifications in job descriptions, and replacing them with skills, abilities, competence, experience *etc.*

Table 4.8 shows the method of recruitment by size of organisation. Notifying the DRO/DEA was more frequently given as a method by companies employing over 200 employees, whilst small companies were more likely to go to the Jobcentre or Careers Office. Specifically worded advertisements were much more frequently used by organisations within the 500 to 4999 and 5000+ bands.

In the postal survey, it was possible to list only a limited number of methods for recruiting people with disabilities. The case studies confirmed that although most organisations did approach either Jobcentres or use the ES services there was a wide range of other methods being employed and revisions of general recruitment practices being made. In the following sub–sections we go on to draw on the case study evidence in this regard.

4.7.1 Advertising

Most case study respondents admitted that at present they were not using advertisements at all because they were not recruiting. Several organisations did indicate that when vacancies did arise they would use specifically worded adverts. Only one case study respondent stated that it used the Employment Service 'double tick symbol'. Most organisations relied on a general equal opportunities statement because they felt that a separate statement about disabilities or an additional symbol as well as the company logo *etc.* was simply too much. Two organisations which indicated on their questionnaire that they used specifically worded advertisements admitted that in practice external advertising is used only for relatively senior or highly skilled jobs which have a much wider geographical catchment area.

Four organisations said that they never advertised because they did not need to. They had so many people writing in anyway, or they found Jobcentres or agencies adequate, or that they regarded the money spent on advertising a waste. Advertisements brought such a massive response that smaller organisations could not cope with the volume. It is not possible, unfortunately, to gauge the extent to which such responses simply reflected the fact that the study was being conducted at a time when the economy had been in deep recession for two years, and when for many employers recruitment and labour turnover were running at historically low levels.

Case Study 4.5 — Electronic Engineering Company

The company has regularly been involved in careers fairs with children from 13 to 15 looking for career opportunities. The Careers Service arrange for representatives from most local colleges and businesses to attend. They are not specifically for young people with disabilities, but some do attend. This year they met a young person who was profoundly deaf. His school did not organise work experience but the Careers Service suggested he should go. They thought the practical experience would help him. As a result of his visit to the fair he was introduced to the personnel officer and she has arranged a work experience placement for six months.

4.7.2 Open days and recruitment fairs

Open days, milkrounds or careers fairs were used by only three case study organisations. Most organisations said that they had so few vacancies that it just was not worth it. Those that had done had mixed success (*case studies numbers 4.5 and 4.6*).

4.7.3 Links with other organisations

Only three of the case study organisations visited had used other bodies in order to recruit people with disabilities. The personnel officer of an electronic engineering company said that they mainly used the ES services but had also been in contact with MENCAP to provide candidates with disabilities, an approach which was judged to have been fairly successful.

> **Case Study 4.6 — Local Authority**
>
> One local authority organised an open day about employing people with disabilities in the council, to which they invited all the government agencies, the Careers Service, voluntary bodies *etc.* as well as people with disabilities. They offered potential disabled applicants advice, including a workshop on how to apply for a job. Unfortunately they felt that the exercise was counterproductive in that it raised the expectations of people attending, for them only to find that there were few or vacancies for them in the current climate.

The other organisation which was mentioned several times was Opportunities for the Disabled. Opportunities is a group which specialises in helping disabled jobseekers find employment through a network of Regional Offices. They act in some ways like an employment agency but also provide advice to employers regarding employing people with disabilities, guidance on special equipment, facilities and adaptations and on sources of financial assistance.

Those organisations which had used Opportunities had found them a helpful and effective means of finding suitable candidates for vacancies (*case study number 4.7*).

> **Case Study 4.7 — Manufacturing Company**
>
> 'We had in the past always used DAS to locate candidates with disabilities, but we have become somewhat disillusioned with the service because they tend to send anyone. As a result we have recently been using the group Opportunities for the Disabled. They seem to be better geared up to the placement of people with disabilities than DAS because their own people spend more time with applicants and often accompany them to interviews.'

4.8 Other recruitment strategies

4.8.1 Training recruitment staff

All the larger organisations interviewed gave training, which covered equal opportunity issues, to all staff who were involved with recruitment or selection training whether they were the personnel officer or line managers. Several personnel managers themselves had found seminars and information provided by the IPM on good practice recruitment and selection extremely useful. Smaller organisations, however, tended to rely on experience gained elsewhere or help from the Employment Service, or other outside bodies such as local Committees/Networks for the Employment of People with Disabilities.

4.8.2 Revising recruitment procedures

Application Forms

There seemed to be some conflict as to whether applications forms should contain questions regarding disability. Some organisations had only just put questions on forms, some had taken advice from the Employment Service and decided to leave them on and others had decided to take them off. The argument for including such questions was that it enabled organisations to monitor the number of applications they received and as well as their recruitment procedures.

Others felt that asking such questions was likely to increase discrimination, would put applicants off, but was also pointless because many people with disabilities would not admit to it on an application form.

New Employee Starter Forms/Interviews

Two organisations, as a result of the conflicts outlined above, preferred to ask applicants about disability and health issues only if they have been successful in their applications, by putting these questions on a new employee form.

Another company asked all new employees to come in for an interview before starting the job. This gives them an opportunity to:

'... chat about the job, to show them around the work area and to double check to see if they feel if there would be any problems either with the work or the work area that may prevent them from doing the job. This even includes asking if they have difficulties with getting to work.' (Electronic engineering company)

4.8.3 Job descriptions

Seven of the case study organisations interviewed were going through some process of re–evaluation of job descriptions and person specifications. In most instances this was not particularly aimed at improving opportunities for people with disabilities but as a general effort towards better practice, or (in two cases) as a requirement for achieving BS5750. The comments below were fairly typical of what was being done:

'The company is now more rigorous when drawing up job descriptions. Every post must have a person specification and the personnel department checks that qualifications asked for are necessary. This is a general policy not just aimed at increasing employment of people with disabilities.' (Manufacturing company)

'We have re–assessed job descriptions and recruitment practices. We have divided all job specifications into the essential and desired qualifications and attributes. This has been done simply as good practice rather than specifically for employing people with disabilities. It is important to be specific about criteria because it makes interviewing more objective.' (Electronic engineering)

'We are developing a good practice guide for managing people with disabilities which will emphasise the message — don't ask for attributes if they are just desirable.' (Financial services organisation)

'As part of the procedure for getting BS5750 it has been necessary to carefully develop person specifications so we do not ask for physical or academic requirements which are unnecessary. The idea is to avoid recruiting people who are simply like ourselves, but open it out to other groups which we may not have though of before.' (R & D group)

One clear trend to emerge in many case studies was the shift from relying on qualification over to an emphasis on skills (*case study number 4.10*).

4.8.4 Guaranteed interview schemes

Guaranteed Interview Schemes (GIS) were run by some organisations either as a part of general good practice or (in one case) because it is to become a 'requirement' for being ES symbol users. The schemes could apply to all vacancies or to just those which the organisation specified as more suitable for people with disabilities; thus, for example, in one organisation the GIS applied only to temporary posts.

Some schemes seemed to run on an informal basis. The GIS in a manufacturing company visited was simply a matter of interviewing anyone who wrote in to the company who indicated that they had a disability. Another organisation said that they did not run a GIS as such, although if a person with a disability has suitable qualifications and meets the job criteria they 'would probably get an interview'.

Other systems were more formal, particularly in the larger organisations and the public sector. One public sector organisation not only operated a guaranteed interview scheme for all disabled, whether registered or not but also stated that all disabled applicants who meet the criteria will be guaranteed a job.

As indicated in section 4.8.2, running a GIS could present some difficulties with regard to removing monitoring questions from applications forms.

4.8.5 Registers of applicants

Very few case study organisations interviewed kept registers specifically of disabled applicants. Often personnel departments would keep all applications for a period of six months. Some however, said that they no longer even did this because they found they just had too many. With the rise in unemployment they had become inundated with letters of application and simply could not hold them all.

One local authority was actually thinking about setting up an employment register of disabled people looking for work, to whom they could send the vacancy lists. The register was to be advertised through the press and community groups and no proof of disability would be required to join (see *case study number 4.4*).

4.8.6 Work experience/training schemes

Work experience schemes were commonly used by case study organisations interviewed and were generally regarded as effective (*case studies 4.11 and 4.12*). The types of schemes range from 'Trident' which provided for two weeks work experience for school children including those with disabilities through to year placements as part of degree courses. Some companies saw work experience as a method of recruiting staff whilst others admitted that there was little chance

Case Study 4.11 — Local Authority

All council departments have been asked to identify posts especially for people with learning difficulties in order that they can get experience of real jobs. This programme is innovative, in that a non–disabled person from the voluntary group operating the programme at first spends some time getting work experience in the jobs in question, and then that person acts as a supervisor for the person with a disability on work experience. This helps get round opposition from hard–pressed line managers who say that they cannot afford to provide the supervision necessary to offer work experience.

They are looking at the work experience area more widely at the moment. In the past they had offered places for school kids, including disabled, under TVEI. They are now looking at doing it systematically for adults; so far these had been on an *ad hoc* basis as a result of requests from voluntary organisations.

of employing them afterwards. Often they were not specifically targeted at people with disabilities, but even in such cases employers argued that they would look particularly favourably on placements for the disabled within their wider scheme.

A minority of such schemes, however did lead to the individuals being kept on after the placement was completed.

> 'We have had some successful work experience schemes. The local branch of the Employment Service set up placements for two boys with learning disabilities (from a special school in the area) to work in the warehouse with guidance. They have been able to keep them on and they are now doing well.' (Wholesale distribution organisation)

Not all work experience was offered with the view to moving on to permanent paid employment if successful. Some schemes were simply set up, for example, to help people complete courses being undertaken at college. One organisation gave a placement to a victim of a traffic accident who was being retrained in office work. He came into the office for a six week period followed by a further two weeks as part of an NVQ course.

Other companies had had mixed experiences with some attempts having been seen as successful and others not. It seemed very much to depend on the individual undertaking the scheme. Two companies found that after the six months offered, the individual concerned simply could not cope with the work either because of deteriorating health or in one case, the individual's 'attitude'.

One organisation said that they did give work experience to people with disabilities but they did not feel that the organisation got much out of it. They liked to 'give people a chance', and felt that so long as they did not have more than one in the firm at any one time it did not affect working practices. The main problem was that the only

Case Study 4.12 — Electronic Engineering Company

Work experience here ranged from 14 to 15 year olds coming in for two weeks on the 'Trident' scheme, to offering work experience to a local college for HNC/HND students, including mature adults. They use work experience for two things:

a) To develop links with schools. They are a source of potential employees who would be interested in careers in the industry. They want to let young people know of the opportunities and training offered. The company ensures that everyone gets training whether they are on YTS, ONC, HNC or Degree Courses.

b) They are also looking to offer work experience at higher levels. They are offering a year's work placement for a higher education student to work in the area/environment of the electronic studio. Students from a local University come for placements. They are also trying to get students to come to them before they start their degrees to get early practical experience.

work they could offer was in their warehouses, where individuals needed constant supervision because of working with fork lift trucks, lorries, heavy crates *etc*. For these reasons they would not keep disabled people on after the placement period.

Only one company stated that they could not use them at all.

'We do not actually have a lot of opportunities for work experience because much of the work requires a lot of training and it's not worth putting that much into someone who will leave after six months or so. We do however, have people from a local college because they tend to seek more realistic types of work, in that the placements are for a much shorter time.' (Financial services organisation)

4.9 Use of government training schemes

The case study interviews (but not the postal survey), asked respondents about their participation in Government Training Schemes (such as Youth Training and Employment Training), and any implications such participation had for employing or offering work placements to trainees with disabilities.

Ten of the twenty one case study organisations were current or past participants in YT (rather fewer had participated in ET), and it was clear (and expected, given the national evidence) that participation had fallen off somewhat in the recession. With only two exceptions, however, participation in these programmes was not seen by case study respondents as having a disability 'angle'. Most said that they did not regard such schemes as a particular source, either of disabled employees, or disabled trainees/work placements; indeed nearly all of them said they had no idea, or record of whether trainees they had had under the schemes were disabled. It is clear, from this small sample of respondents at least, that employers did not view these programmes, for the most part as providing a potential source of disabled recruits.

One electronics company did, however, report that it had used YT and ET and had taken several disabled trainees on both trainee status placements, and as employees. In practice, however they were only occasionally able to take any of these staff on to the permanent payroll:

'... as we discussed, we have used both YT and ET, with some of the placements being for disabled people. Andrew came to the company on YT; he had suffered a stroke at birth and so had very limited mobility down one side, especially in his arm. After his placement ended we were keen to keep him on; his motivation was good, but his productivity was only around 60 per cent of what we achieve from other staff. The DRO suggested we look into the Sheltered Placement Scheme, and he has subsequently gone on to work with us through REMPLOY. We also had a driver who came to us through ET, and who turned out to have epilepsy; he was moved into administration, but eventually his health deteriorated and he left ...'

A research and development company had taken a disabled woman through 'an adult YOPS scheme' (which turned out to be ET on further questioning); she was a woman returner with a 'very nervous disposition'; after a trial period of work experience, she was taken on full time. On another occasion, however, they were less successful:

'... we took a person on one of these schemes, after being approached by [...] college for a work placement. He had severe mental illness, although he was very bright. He was given a fairly menial job, booking in samples, and describing the product. He started off very well, but something then went wrong, perhaps with his medication. We kept reducing his work burden, but he eventually cracked up, and by Christmas he could hardly do anything, not even make coffee. He had no support from Social Services, and we eventually got him admitted to hospital... '

4.10 The Employment Service disability symbol

Respondents to the postal survey who stated that their organisation actively sought to recruit people with disabilities, were also asked whether they used the Employment Service ('double tick') disability symbol in their job advertisements and recruitment literature. Of the 206 organisations responding to this question, only 65 (or 32 per cent) did so, and nearly all of these were drawn from the 'good practice' sub–sample (unsurprisingly), since use of the symbol had been one of the criteria for drawing the sample. Given the small numbers involved, detailed breakdown of symbol users by size and sector is not meaningful, but it would seem, firstly, that use of the symbol was more widespread among service sector (except for distribution) and energy/water supply organisations than among manufacturing and construction organisations. Further, as might be expected, users were concentrated among larger organisations (49 of the 65 had 500 or more employees).

Use/non–use of the symbol was explored in the case study interviews (a quarter of whom were users), and several perspectives emerged.

At one extreme were a minority of organisations, who although generally proactive in their policies towards employing people with disabilities, did not use the symbol. Some even argued that use might be counterproductive for that particular organisation.

> 'We do not use the symbol, although we know all about it and have considered it. Our Disability Officer sees it as a PR exercise, and argues that we should simply stick with our clear existing EO statement, which goes on all our advertising material, and is explicit about our approach to people with disabilities. His view is that if we cover our publicity material with razzmatazz saying how good we are on disability, we end up looking as if we are over–doing it, and may even have something to hide!' (Local authority)

Other non–users felt less strongly:

> 'We don't use it, because we don't really advertise. We usually go through Jobcentres and agencies. We have too many logos to go on our letter heads as it is. We think it's better to have a wider EO banner, rather than to just highlight disability.' (Electronics company)

Some organisations used the symbol (because they saw themselves as 'good practice' organisations), but nevertheless saw problems with it:

> 'The point of the symbol is that it's supposed to be a simple way of communicating a positive attitude to recruiting disabled people, thereby replacing the need to put a lot of words to this effect in job adverts. In practice, however, how successful it is in doing this depends very much on ES's marketing, which we suspect has not been very effective to date — most people have no idea what the two ticks mean, and even if they know, for example, that it's something to do with disabled people, they certainly don't know that it means they are guaranteed an interview. We are relying on the tick symbol to communicate this policy to the labour market, but are afraid that it doesn't. We recognise that the new text around the symbol is supposed to make it clearer ('positive about disabled people'). We haven't gone to all the expense of changing all our literature to accommodate this, however, since we have also noticed that much of the other stuff which ES puts out says we should use the term 'people with disabilities'. The last thing we want is to get everything printed, and then have to change it again, when the ES realise that their symbol isn't politically correct. Despite all this, however, we have signed up to the new 'tightened up' symbol with its five commitments, and we regard it (in personnel) as useful, since it gives us a lever for being more proactive within the company on disability issues. We can, for example, insist that line managers give all disabled people a discussion about their needs at least once a year, because we tell them that the company has publicly committed itself to this.' (Financial services organisation)

Some users who regarded themselves as good practice, were afraid that the lack of enforcement of the symbol's criteria might eventually result in some users being discovered by disabled workers, and their lobby organisations, as not living up to the symbol, with the effect that those users who rigorously kept to the criteria might be 'tainted' as a result:

> 'We do use the symbol, although I'm a bit sceptical about its usefulness. It certainly doesn't do any harm, and its eligibility criteria have certainly improved, but it is self–policing, and the ES never check (*eg* whether all users operate a guaranteed interview scheme). It's better than nothing but I can think of better ways of helping disabled people.' (Financial services organisation)

> 'The symbol is too easy to get, just by saying you meet the criteria. It's not like *Investors in People* for example, which is very difficult to get, but if an employer has it, it really means they have made strides forward. ... A further problem, I think, is that the general public are not yet aware of it. It's not really obvious, just looking at it, what it's all about.' (Local authority)

At the other extreme some users, and intended users of the symbol were unambiguously positive about it. In one case study, for example, the personnel officer stated:

> 'We've found out all about the symbol, and are aiming to achieve double tick status soon. It will be useful for us, because it will show people (not just disabled ones) the kind of company they are coming into.' (Manufacturing company)

> 'We use it, and think it works well, now that people are beginning to understand what it means. It tells the disabled that we are a disability–friendly company, and more generally it has public relations benefits for us. It has improved recently, now that users are under greater pressure to comply with certain criteria such as a Guaranteed Interview Scheme'. (Manufacturing company)

5. The 'Pros' and 'Cons' of Employing People with Disabilities

5.1 Introduction

This chapter looks at the benefits that employers see associated with the employment of people with disabilities, and at any problems and difficulties employers experience in recruiting and employing people with disabilities.

5.2 Advantages of employing people with disabilities

The traditional emphasis of much discussion about the employment of people with disabilities has been very much on disability as causing problems or difficulties for the employer, or acting as a barrier to employment. It is also clearly of interest, however, to establish what (if any) benefits or advantages organisations believe they derive from recruiting and employing people with disabilities. This can have important policy implications for strategies of 'marketing' people with disabilities to potential employers.

To redress this balance, therefore, the postal survey also asked respondents whether they saw any benefit or advantage to the organisation associated with the recruitment or employment of people with disabilities. Some 1,100 respondents answered this question, of whom only 314 (28.5 per cent) said they did see such benefits or advantages (48 per cent said they did not, and 24 per cent did not know).

Relating these results to whether or not an organisation has employees with disabilities we find that considerably more employers of people with disabilities (42 per cent) see such advantages, compared with those who do not employ disabled people, of whom only 11 per cent see advantages in it. Taking these results at face value, nevertheless, they would seem to imply that at least a half of those who employ people with disabilities do not see any advantage in it (and presumably *either* they do not distinguish between people with and without disabilities in this sense, *or* they employ people with disabilities for primarily altruistic or social reasons).

Perception of these benefits was also strongly related to organisational size, increasing steadily from seven per cent of the smallest firms in the 1 to 10 employee size band, to 75 per cent in the 5,000–plus employee band.

Finally, respondents were asked to give brief details of the advantages and benefits they saw in employing people with disabilities, and Table 5.1 summarises their comments, confirming in broad terms the strong role of 'social responsibility' related factors (around half of those identifying benefits saw a strong role for social and equal opportunities issues).

Table 5.1 Perceived advantages in employing people with disabilities

Advantage	% of employers identifying benefits who cited specified advantage
Social responsibility/equal opportunities	50.3
More committed workforce	43.3
Wider recruitment field	20.1
Raising awareness	15.3
Promotes team spirit	7.0
Fulfil legal obligations	1.0
Financial support	0.6
Unspecified	1.9
TOTAL (N=)	314

Population of Table (n) is all respondents perceiving advantages in employing people with disabilities

Source: IMS Survey

This is not to say, of course that respondents did not also recognise the 'business benefits' of employing people with disabilities — thus, for example, 43 per cent cited the benefit of a more committed workforce, and a further 20 per cent believed that the employment of people with disabilities offered them a wider recruitment field (it is likely that this proportion would have been higher, but for the recessionary circumstances prevailing in the labour market at the time of the study).

Written responses on the survey questionnaire and comments made in interviews with organisations regarding the advantages of employing people with disabilities tended to fall into two broad areas. A large number of respondents highlighted the advantages gained through the motivation and dedication of the individual employee with the disability, whilst many others felt advantages were gained through an enhanced image of the company to both other employees and customers.

On the question of employee quality, the following are typical quotes from the survey:

'Our experience has shown that disabled people are hard working; value their jobs; are usually able to overcome potential "barriers", and do not take as much time off due to sickness as some of our "able bodied" employees.' (Financial services company)

'They are on the whole more enthusiastic about employment and are more flexible than most.' (Automotive manufacturing company)

'Having the skills and experience the person has to offer in the company helps to change attitudes and awareness of abilities of disabled people to the rest of the workforce.' (Energy and water company)

'Our MD has serious mobility problems as a result of a road accident. His example of dedication and commitment in difficult conditions are a driving force in the success of his company.' (Bulk haulage company)

'Disabled people may be less likely to move from job to job, offering stability and loyalty to their employer provided they are not abused.' (Financial services company)

'Disabilities do not make an employee a lesser person. As a rule they tend to be extremely loyal.' (Coach operator)

'Our experience is that disabled employees tend to be good, committed workers and are keen to please.' (Printing company)

'People with disabilities bring their own talents and ambition to the company. Often they try harder than other employees. They can also help the company understand the needs of customers with disabilities.' (Communications company)

'Allows individuals to develop their talents without barriers. Continuation of employment of people who become disabled secures the skill and investment of a tried and trusted employee.' (Energy and water company)

The question of company image was also raised in many of the questionnaires and in case–study interviews (*see case study number 5.1*). Population of Table (n) is all respondents perceiving advantages in employing people with disabilities. This was summed up by the equal opportunities manager of a financial services company when asked about their motivation for employing people with disabilities:

'The motivation is really the same as the reasons given for having an equal opportunities policy. It was thought that if we have a diverse workforce it reflects the community at large and is good for business. People have a wide range of skills and we need to use them all. Also we feel that graduates tend to look for companies with good equal opportunities because it implies their chances of promotion will be better.'

There were many other examples of organisations whose views about employing people with disabilities rested on a mix of social and business advantages:

> **Case Study 5.1 — Financial Services**
>
> A large company in the financial services sector was trying to link its approach to people with disabilities amongst employees to its approach to customer care. This involved being seen as friendly to people with disabilities. Customer leverage was thought important in convincing managers to change their views, and since it had worked with ethnic minorities and women so it should work with disabled. The basis for this was that they would be able to attract more customers with disabilities as by being seen as a disability-friendly organisation, in which the employment of people with disabilities plays an important part.

'The motivation for it all was really a mixture of company policy and community profile. We feel that you should do your bit. The local community does us well, we are a successful business and we feel we should do our bit for them.' (Electrical engineering company)

'The motivation is mostly to improve the view that the employees will have of the company. It helps with staff retention. Also there is an element of social responsibility.' (Electronic engineering company)

'We employ people with disabilities to capitalise on resources and skills available; to help and to reflect all sectors of the community; the disabled are our customers.' (Retail company)

'As a local authority, employing a mix of people from the population sends a powerful message to our "customers". As a social services authority, we also need to extend care and concern in practical realistic ways.' (Local authority)

5.3 Reservations about the recruitment of people with disabilities

Moving to the more 'negative' aspects of employer perceptions, respondents were asked what questions or reservations would be uppermost in their mind if a person with a disability applied for a job. The question was designed not so much to identify experienced problems, but to elicit a more subjective response from the respondents about their attitude to disabled job applicants. The most commonly reported reservation concerned the applicant's ability to do the job and their level of productivity, with 56 per cent of respondents citing this reservation. Behind this were concerns over the safety of both the individual and other employees (11 per cent), access to and safety around the premises (seven per cent), and the mobility of the applicant (six per cent). Other commonly reported reservations were the special needs or requirements for the applicant, and their timekeeping or absence from work. Extra costs were rarely seen as a concern, with fewer than one per cent of respondents reporting this reservation.

Table 5.2 Reservations about recruiting people with disabilities by sector

Disability	All	Energy/ Water	Metals/ Minerals	Engin- eering	Other Manuf.	Constr- uction	Distrib./ Hotels	Transport / Comms.	Business services	Other Services
				% of employers in sector with reservations about people with disability						
Special needs	4.0	16.0	2.8	4.1	3.0	3.1	3.2	1.1	6.0	3.5
Job ability	56.1	52.0	62.0	54.3	56.7	48.4	56.1	60.2	53.3	60.3
Absence	3.4	0.0	1.4	5.6	0.0	3.1	5.8	1.1	4.3	1.4
Medical care	0.2	4.0	0.0	0.5	0.0	0.0	0.0	0.0	0.0	0.0
Extra costs	0.4	0.0	0.0	1.0	1.5	0.0	0.0	0.0	0.0	0.7
Safety of individual	10.6	4.0	16.9	16.2	20.9	17.2	11.0	4.3	4.3	5.0
Driving restrictions	1.4	0.0	0.0	2.0	1.5	1.6	0.6	3.2	1.6	0.7
Mobility	5.7	8.0	0.0	5.6	4.5	6.3	5.2	7.5	7.1	6.4
Customer attitudes	0.3	0.0	0.0	0.0	0.0	0.0	0.6	0.0	0.5	0.7
Effect on staff	1.2	0.0	1.4	0.5	0.0	0.0	0.6	3.2	1.6	2.1
Mental attitude	0.8	0.0	0.0	0.0	0.0	0.0	0.6	1.1	1.6	2.1
Premises and access	7.0	4.0	7.0	4.1	1.5	7.8	7.1	7.5	10.3	9.2
Depends on disability	5.8	8.0	5.6	5.1	6.0	7.8	5.8	5.4	6.0	5.7
Depends on job	1.4	4.0	0.0	0.5	3.0	3.1	1.9	2.2	1.6	0.0
Other	1.6	0.0	2.8	0.5	1.5	1.6	1.3	3.3	1.5	2.1
N=	998	25	71	197	67	64	155	93	184	141

Population of Table (n) is all respondents in sample

Note: Sector SIC 0 Agriculture, Forestry and Fishing was not included — see Appendix 1, Section 1.2

Source: IMS Survey

Table 5.2 shows these reservations broken down by sector. Concerns over job ability and productivity were most evident in the metals and minerals sector, other services, and transport and communication. Questions about the safety of the individual were most frequently reported in the manufacturing sectors and in construction, while the most concern about access to the premises was found among organisations in the business and other services sectors. There were no clear patterns by size in the types of reservations reported by respondents, although questions about job ability and productivity were most evident among the larger organisations with over 500 employees.

Institute of Manpower Studies

Most of the organisations interviewed in the case studies did not express any reservations regarding employing people with disabilities. Those which did were mainly regarding health and safety aspects of the working environment in which they had to operate. This was particularly important in smaller companies where it was difficult to ensure that an individual would not have to work in a dangerous or physically demanding area. The personnel director of a retail distribution company pointed out that most of their work was physical.

> 'The most obvious problem facing the company with regard to the employment of people with disabilities is the physical nature of a lot of the jobs. Even if not recruited specifically to do lifting jobs, all staff very often have to "muck in" and help out if short staffed or have large numbers of orders, or customers need boxes carrying to their cars.'

Very similar comments were made by the managing director of a small construction company visited. His major reservation regarding people with disabilities was whether they would have the physical fitness required to work on a building site. The health and safety requirements were very strict and not only could an individual be a danger to himself but could very easily endanger others. The same applied to the company interviewed which provided laboratory services to the consumer industry. Any staff working in the laboratory had to meet their health and safety requirements.

There was only one case study in which the respondent felt that people with disabilities in general had problems working. He had experienced difficulties with one member of staff and as a result was not prepared to take on any others. He was under the impression that they tended to be lazy because they received too many state benefits and were not really prepared to work.

5.4 Problems experienced in employment of people with disabilities

Moving from perception to experience, our survey asked whether employers had experienced any particular problems or difficulties in the employment of people with disabilities. This experience did not appear to be widespread among the sample. Of the 1,101 respondents that answered this question, 17 per cent replied that they had experienced some difficulties employing people with disabilities, while 72 per cent of respondents said they had not experienced any problems and 11 per cent replied that they did not know. These figures, however, include respondents who did not employ people with disabilities and were therefore unlikely to have experienced such problems; if we take simply those who currently employ people with disabilities, the proportion of those who had experienced problems rises to 26 per cent (out of 625), but this still leaves three quarters of all those who employed people with disabilities having experienced no particular problems in doing so.

Among those with no disabled employees, there was a small minority (five per cent) who claimed to have experienced problems in employing people with disabilities. Presumably these are

Table 5.3 Experience of problems in employing people with disabilities

| | %| | | |
	Yes	No	Don't Know	N=
Total	**17.0**	**71.8**	**11.3**	**1,101**
Sector				
Energy/Water supply	33.3	48.1	18.5	27
Metals/Minerals	17.3	73.3	9.3	75
Engineering	17.5	73.1	9.4	212
Other Manufacturing	20.0	74.3	5.7	70
Construction	16.9	69.0	14.1	71
Distribution/Hotels	12.3	78.8	8.9	179
Transport/Communication	11.1	76.9	12.0	108
Financial and Business Services	20.1	68.3	11.6	199
Other Services	17.5	66.3	16.3	160
Number of employees				
1 – 10	5.8	82.5	11.7	206
11 – 49	8.1	82.8	9.1	198
50 – 199	16.7	73.3	10.0	221
200 – 499	21.5	67.2	11.3	186
500 – 4999	29.5	60.9	9.6	156
5000+	30.8	49.5	19.8	91

Population of Table (n) is all respondents in sample

Note: Sector SIC 0 Agriculture, Forestry and Fishing was not included — see Appendix 1, Section 1.2

Source: IMS Survey

employing people with disabilities. Presumably these are organisations which once did, but no longer employ disabled people.

Table 5.3 looks at the incidence of these problems by sector and size of organisation. There are some clear sectoral variations — the energy and water supply sector along with other manufacturing and financial and business services are most likely to have experienced problems. The distribution, hotels and catering sector and transport and communication have the lowest proportion of organisations that have experienced difficulties. A third of organisations in the energy and water supply sector, and a fifth of those in the other manufacturing, have experienced some difficulties in the employment of people with disabilities, while fewer than one in eight employers in distribution and hotels and transport and communication have experienced such problems.

Given the large variation in the sizes of organisations between the sectors, these differences may merely be a size effect. Table 5.3 shows that there is a strong size effect, with the likelihood of having experienced problems increasing with the size of the organisation. Only six per cent of organisations with ten or less employees have experienced difficulties, while this proportion rises to three in ten for organisations with 500 or more employees. These size influences are likely to be responsible for the high incidence of problems in the energy and water supply sector, and the low incidence in transport and communication, although the size compositions of the other manufacturing sector, distribution and hotels, and financial and business services, show no strong bias to either the largest or smallest organisations.

Given the increasing propensity with size to employ disabled workers, however, a more valid test of whether the likelihood of experiencing problems varies with size or type of firm is to look only at those employers who currently employ people with disabilities. Table 5.4 does this.

Table 5.4 Experience of problems in employing people with disabilities

	%			
	Yes	No	Don't Know	N=
Total	**25.8**	**65.3**	**9.0**	**625**
Sector				
Energy/Water supply	33.3	50.0	16.7	24
Metals/Minerals	21.4	67.9	10.7	56
Engineering	25.9	69.6	4.4	135
Other Manufacturing	28.0	68.0	4.0	50
Construction	25.0	59.4	15.6	32
Distribution/Hotels	14.7	74.7	10.5	95
Transport/Communication	22.7	65.9	11.4	44
Financial and Business Services	35.2	56.5	8.3	108
Other Services	27.2	61.7	11.1	81
Number of employees				
1 – 10	19.4	80.6	0.0	31
11 – 49	16.4	82.0	1.6	61
50 – 199	22.3	70.0	7.7	130
200 – 499	26.1	64.8	9.2	142
500 – 4999	30.2	62.4	7.4	149
5000+	30.8	49.5	19.8	91

Population of Table (n) is all respondents currently employing people with disabilities

Note: Sector SIC 0 Agriculture, Forestry and Fishing was not included — see Appendix 1, Section 1.2

Source: IMS Survey

More than a quarter of organisations that employ people with disabilities have experienced difficulties in employing disabled workers, compared with 17 per cent for all organisations. The financial and business services sector has the highest incidence of problems with disabled employees among organisations that employ people with disabilities, and generally the size and sectoral disabled workers compared with all organisations. The size effect nevertheless remains, and among employers who employ disabled people the proportion experiencing difficulties tends to increase with size. Given that larger organisations are more likely to have a clear policy on employing people with disabilities, and more likely to take a proactive stance in recruitment, it is of course possible that this increasing incidence of problems with size reflects a greater likelihood or willingness on the part of such employers to recruit the more severely disabled (and subsequently to deal with any 'problems' this might generate).

5.4.1 Types of problems and disabilities affected

Respondents who replied that they had experienced problems or difficulties in the employment of people with disabilities were further asked to indicate the nature of the problem or difficulty, and the disability in question. Table 5.5 shows the difficulties which our respondents have experienced in the employment of people with disabilities. The most common difficulty experienced was inability to do the job and low productivity, cited by a quarter of respondents, which as we saw above was the most common concern of employers regarding disabled job seekers. Following this were attitude and temperament problems and mobility problems, each cited by around 15 per cent of respondents, and accommodation problems (ie access to lifts, toilets, and other facilities) reported by 12 per cent of respondents. Other common problems were that disabled employees were often unreliable and had frequent time off, that the job required manual labour, finding other suitable employment in the organisation, and safety factors.

Examples of these problems were also given during the case study interviews, and in what follows we consider some of the responses.

Inability to do the job

There were several cases of employees who had become ill and although every effort was made to keep them on, their worsening condition eventually made them so disabled it was impossible to continue to do the job (*see case study number 5.2*).

Case Study 5.2 — Financial Services

There were cases where they could not keep someone on. One particular woman developed severe rheumatoid arthritis, which was very erratic and sometimes very bad. This severely limited the job she could do and the length of time she could work. It was clear that this was going to be a lifetime problem which was going to get gradually worse. In the end they had to retire her on grounds of ill health.

Table 5.5 Difficulties experienced in the employment of people

Difficulty	% of employers with difficulties citing difficulty in question
Inability to do job/low productivity	24.1
Attitude/temperament problem	15.5
Mobility	13.9
Access to facilities	11.8
Manual labour	10.7
Safety	10.2
Absence/timekeeping	9.6
Redeployment/flexibility	9.1
Communication	8.0
Dealing with hazardous materials	4.3
Access to equipment	4.3
Emergency evacuation	4.3
Attracting disabled staff	4.3
Manager prejudice	3.2
Inability to work alone	3.2
Effect on other staff	2.7
Constant standing	1.6
Providing medical aid	1.6
Steady deterioration	1.6
Work in confined area	1.1
Provision of equipment through PACT	1.1
Passing medical examination	1.1
Delays by DAS regarding assistance	0.5
Modifying cars, equipment, *etc.*	0.5
Problems with career progression	0.5
Requirement to work from home	0.5
Unspecified	2.1
TOTAL (N=)	187

Population of Table (n) is all respondents who have experienced problems in the employment of people with disabilities

Source: IMS Survey

There were also cases where the disability of a new employee proved too severe for the individual to cope with the work they were employed to do. A electrical engineering company had a great deal of difficulty with one of their work experience placements:

'We had someone who was autistic on a trial for six months but he turned out to be a nightmare. I spent half of my time trying to sort him out. It took six months setting up the job and we actually employed someone to sit with him but he just could not cope in the end.'

Attitude of employees with disability

Some case study organisations that had had bad experiences with people with disabilities, claimed that these related to the attitude of the individual, and that this attitude was in some way associated with, or resulted from the disability itself (and therefore, by implication, was different from attitude problems encountered in able–bodied employees). An electronic engineering company interviewed for the study took a person on who had diabetes and was in a wheelchair. He constantly took time off without any notice even though he was given all the time he wanted for hospital visits and had all his physiotherapy treatment paid for him by the company. He then became extremely dissatisfied after a dispute over a training scheme which further exacerbated the situation and eventually he left without any warning.

There were also several examples of companies experiencing difficulties because of the attitude of existing employees. A personnel manager from a financial institution was facing the difficulty of a member of staff who was refusing help although he desperately needed it. This particular member of staff who has retinitis pigmentosis, has deteriorating sight and will eventually go blind. The employer wants to find a suitable place for him and provide the right equipment and training before he goes blind. They have talked to the ES about it, but they are unable to do anything until he goes for an assessment by the RNIB. He has so far refused to go, because he can not face his problem.

Attitudes of people with disabilities were also sometimes seen to be a problem when an employee had been off sick a long time. One example was from another electrical engineering company:

'Someone had a broken back so we bought him a computer so he could re–learn his skills. He was originally a maintenance electrician but whilst he was at home recovering he re–trained in electronics and design. It has been nearly three years now and he still has not returned to work. It is not that he can not physically do the work, it seems that whilst ill he has developed a mental problem.'

Problems were also faced by organisations trying to redeploy people with disabilities into other jobs because they did not like the only other work that was available to them. This was typified by the comments made by the equal opportunities manager of a large company in the transport and communications sector:

'Back strain and injuries are common amongst engineers. It used to be possible to put them on to light duties but this is being phased out. They are now being encouraged to re–train as clerical operatives. In some instances the difference between the jobs is not as great as the titles would imply. Clerical operatives take details of faults or problems and it is useful to have some technical background. It is however, perceived as being a demotion. In addition clerical work is seen as being a female preserve. This has led to an enormous amount of dissatisfaction.'

Accommodation problems

As mentioned in Section 3.6 many organisations said they have difficulties with the premises they operate from, especially if they tend to have many outlets in high streets or main shopping locations. A financial services organisation had many of its offices in buildings which either belonged to English Heritage or had strict planning constraints. This made it very difficult to get permission to make physical alterations especially to the outside of a building.

Both local authorities interviewed stated that the buildings they operated from presented problems in both attracting and employing people with disabilities.

One found a major problem was a question of image. The main council building was very old and situated on the side of a hill. Although this is inaccessible to many people with disabilities the council had numerous other sites which were more accessible, but because most people associated the council with the main site they would not apply for jobs with them. To overcome problems of staff having to visit the main building, for example to see the personnel and training department, they now sent trainers out to remote sites if necessary.

Making internal alterations could also prove costly, especially if it involved major changes such as installing a lift. The case study below (*case study number 5.3*) clearly illustrates difficulties companies face.

Case Study 5.3 — Electronic Engineering Company

Their main problem encountered was that they could not put in a lift. Their personnel and training offices with the open learning facilities are all on the first floor of the older building. There had been plans to move these functions into the new office building but it was felt that it may distance personnel too much from the staff if they were isolated away from production. They also found that there was not adequate room there.

To overcome the mobility problems of the stairs to the first floor, they looked into installing a lift. All they wanted was a home lift with a special key that only disabled staff could have access to. It was refused because they were not allowed to install a domestic lift in a commercial environment. The alternative was to use a factory lift which was far too heavy duty for their requirements and would have cost them three times the amount of the domestic lift. They simply could not afford it. To run courses they now have to carry all the equipment down to the ground floor which tends to make disabled staff feel uncomfortable. They had thought of moving Personnel to the ground floor but decided they could not because this is seen as prime activity space for manufacturing functions.

Further problems from case studies

Despite the enthusiasm of most organisations interviewed for employing people with disabilities, they had often faced other problems not mentioned in survey responses. These varied a great deal and were generally not caused by the actual disability itself, but stemmed from a wide range of sources such as management attitudes and economic circumstances.

Case Study 5.4 — Local Authority

Local authorities seem to be facing particular problems, especially because of Compulsory Competitive Tendering (or CCT) as illustrated by this case study:

'One of the reasons for the decline in people with disabilities throughout the council is due to spending cuts and resulting staff reductions. Due to the need to make voluntary redundancies, people who can take ill–health retirement are often quite keen to leave because they get a good package. This is not discouraged by the council because money comes from the superannuation fund and does not cost them redundancy pay. The members of staff who are eligible for this tend to be older, in higher grades and with more experience.

'There have also been problems relating to CCT. Now with budgets so tight and no control over outside contractors, the opportunities for people with disabilities are diminishing. It is also no longer possible to transfer staff as easily. Previously, staff who became disabled in a manual job would have been transferred to a department which had more sedentary work. CCT areas are now more hard–nosed about how long they will look for alternative work and how long they keep someone on after the sick pay runs out. A few years ago it was unheard of to get rid of someone before sick pay was exhausted but now it happens because heads of department say they can not afford to pay someone sick pay and also pay extra for someone else to cover for them. Finally, the council now has a new management culture of cost centres and departments controlling their own budgets. They have also become less receptive to people with disabilities because of fears over costs.'

As a result of these changes the council has had two members of staff who have become disabled, one with arthritis and another with an eye problem, and has been unable to find alternative work for either. One has now had to accept early retirement on grounds of ill health.

Attitudes of management and other personnel

Case study organisations frequently felt that a barrier to employing or retaining a person with a disability was due to the traditional approach of management staff. The employee relations manager of a manufacturing company felt that:

'There haven't been any problems with actual changes to work or technology. The real difficulty is getting people and managers to have the initiative. They need to encourage managers to be more imaginative about employing people with disabilities.'

A personnel officer from a local authority had similar problems:

> '... the greatest difficulty I come across is an individual manager's prejudice against someone with the label "disabled".'

Economic circumstances

Economic factors were also often cited as a creating further problems with the employment of people with disabilities in both the public and private sector. Most organisations that were not recruiting or were experiencing reductions in staff found that this seriously restricted the opportunities for employing new members of staff with disabilities, but also and more distressingly, hampered efforts to retain staff (*see case study 5.4*).

These sorts of problems were not confined to the public sector. A large financial services organisation faced similar problems.

> 'Economic circumstances mean that the branches are now under a lot of pressure. There is only so much other staff could take on to restructure work for a person with a disability, especially since there are far fewer back office jobs. Nearly all the staff have to serve on the counter because of rationalisations. In addition there are fewer outlets so again less options. If an individual has limited mobility they cannot be sent to a branch a long way away. Also, if they wanted to work part–time or on a job share it can be difficult to arrange with the very low staff turnover we are now experiencing.'

5.4.2 Most common disabilities causing problems

Table 5.6 shows that the most common disability with which difficulties arose was mobility problems, with two in five respondents citing this. This was followed by hearing (with one in eight respondents reporting this disability) and epilepsy, being wheelchair bound, and seeing, each cited by around one in ten respondents. Sixteen per cent of respondents replied that various disabilities brought about the problem in question.

In order to examine which disabilities cause which problems, we have aggregated some of the categories used above to reduce the complexity of the resulting table. Looking first at the disabilities, wheelchair bound, loss of limb and lack of manual dexterity have been combined with mobility, problems with seeing, hearing, and speaking have been combined to create a new 'sensory impairment' category, depression and bad nerves have been combined with mental handicaps, and various and other disabilities have formed the 'other' category. Among the difficulties and problems, dealing with hazardous materials and providing emergency aid have been combined with the safety category, access to equipment and emergency evacuation have been combined with the access to facilities category, manager prejudice has been combined with effects on staff, constant standing has been combined with mobility, and the 'other' category has been formed from steady deterioration, delays by DAS, inability to work alone, attracting disabled staff, passing medical examinations and problems with career progression.

Table 5.6 Disabilities causing problems in employment

Disability	% of employers with difficulties citing disability in question
Mobility	39.6
Hearing difficulty	12.3
Seeing difficulty	9.1
Allergy/skin condition	3.2
Heart and circulation problems	6.4
Chest and breathing problems	5.3
Epilepsy	11.2
Diabetes	3.7
Digestion (stomach, liver, bladder *etc.*)	1.6
Depression/bad nerves	2.7
Mental illness	1.6
Mental handicap	8.0
Drug/alcohol dependency	2.1
Wheelchair bound	10.7
Deaf without speech	1.1
Speech impairment	1.1
Loss of limb/amputee	4.8
Lack of manual dexterity	2.1
Various	15.5
Other/unspecified	10.2
TOTAL (N=)	187

Population of Table (n) is all respondents who have experienced problems in the employment of people with disabilities

Source: IMS Survey

The patterns between the disabilities in question and the problems encountered are shown in Table 5.7. Employees with disabilities affecting mobility (including being wheelchair bound, those with lost limbs and lack of manual dexterity) brought about considerable problems regarding mobility around the premises, access to facilities and equipment, and manual labour intensive jobs. Sensory impairment and mental handicap were a disproportionately large influence bringing about job ability and productivity problems, and were the sole cause of communication problems. Allergies and skin conditions caused problems regarding safety and hazardous materials in the workplace, while epilepsy caused similar safety problems and also caused problems among other employees. There is little consistent variation in the problems associated with employing disabled people by employment size or by sector, although problems regarding safety and hazardous materials were more prevalent among organisations in the production industries.

Table 5.7 Patterns of problems and the disabilities that cause them

| Problem | % of Employers Citing Disability Causing Specific Problem | | | | | | | | | | |
	All	Mo-bility	Senses	Allergy	Heart	Brea-thing	Epi-lepsy	Dia-betes	Mental Disorder	Other/ Various	N=
All	100.0	41.4	15.5	2.3	2.9	2.9	9.2	2.9	7.5	15.5	174
Job ability	16.7	24.1	27.6	0.0	6.9	3.4	10.3	0.0	13.8	13.8	29
Attitude	11.5	55.0	15.0	0.0	0.0	0.0	5.0	5.0	5.0	15.0	20
Mobility	12.1	81.0	0.0	0.0	4.8	0.0	9.5	0.0	0.0	4.8	21
Manual labour	5.7	70.0	0.0	0.0	0.0	0.0	0.0	10.0	0.0	20.0	10
Absence	6.3	27.3	9.1	0.0	9.1	18.2	0.0	18.2	0.0	18.2	11
Access	14.4	80.0	12.0	0.0	4.0	0.0	0.0	0.0	0.0	4.0	25
Communication	4.6	0.0	87.5	0.0	0.0	0.0	0.0	0.0	12.5	0.0	8
Safety	9.8	5.9	5.9	23.5	0.0	5.9	29.4	5.9	11.8	11.8	17
Redeployment	5.2	44.4	11.1	0.0	0.0	11.1	11.1	0.0	11.1	11.1	9
Effect on staff	3.4	0.0	16.7	0.0	0.0	0.0	33.3	0.0	16.7	33.3	6
Other	10.3	11.1	11.1	0.0	0.0	0.0	11.1	0.0	16.7	50.0	18

Population of Table (n) is all respondents who have experienced problems in the employment of people with disabilities

Source: IMS Survey

5.5 Disabilities as a barrier to employment

Our respondents were asked if they felt there were specific disabilities which would *prevent* a person being employed in the organisation (as opposed to just generating difficulties for the organisation). More than half of our 1,081 respondents that answered this question (570, or 53 per cent) replied that certain disabilities would be a barrier to employment, while 24 per cent said that disabilities would not be a barrier and 23 per cent said they did not know. There appeared to be no significant size or sectoral variation in the answers to this question. Table 5.8 looks at the disabilities which were cited as a potential barrier to employment in the organisation.

The largest category of disabilities that would prevent someone being employed is the broad group of disabilities affecting mobility and dexterity, with over two thirds of respondents perceiving these disabilities as a barrier to employment. Following mobility problems are the two sensory disabilities, seeing problems, cited by just under a third of respondents, and hearing problems, cited by one in six respondents. Epilepsy and mental handicaps are also commonly perceived to limit employment prospects. Blood disorders and problems with the digestive system, which as we saw in Chapter 2

Table 5.8 Disabilities which would prevent employment in the organisation

Disability	% of employers citing disability in question as a barrier
Mobility/dexterity (incl. wheelchair)	67.9
Hearing difficulty (incl. deaf without speech)	16.3
Seeing difficulty	31.1
Allergy/skin condition	5.1
Heart and circulation problems	4.9
Chest and breathing problems	4.0
Epilepsy	11.2
Diabetes	1.1
Digestion (stomach, liver, bladder *etc.*)	0.4
Blood disorders	0.4
Depression/nerves/anxiety	3.9
Mental illness	6.7
Mental handicap/learning disorders	11.4
Drug/alcohol dependency	7.9
Speech impairment	2.3
Various	15.8
Other/unspecified	5.8
TOTAL (N=)	570

Population of Table (n) is all respondents indicating specific disabilities are a barrier to employment

Source: IMS Survey

are not uncommon disabilities among employees, are rarely seen as a barrier to employment.

Table 5.9 takes the analysis further by matching the specific disabilities that are perceived to be barriers to employment with the reasons why it is believed that they would prevent employment.

Most of the patterns between the disabilities and the reasons are obvious and intuitive — use of the telephone being a barrier for those with hearing difficulties and speech impairments; computers, VDUs and paperwork preventing those with seeing difficulties being employed, and the layout of the premises hindering employment opportunities for those with mobility problems.

Table 5.9 Barriers to employment posed by specific disabilities

Problem	% of employers citing specific problem, by disability										
	All	Mobility	Wheel-chair	Hearing	Seeing	Heart	Breath-ing	Epilepsy	Mental Disorder	Other/ Various	N=
All	**100.0**	**36.6**	**12.3**	**5.9**	**15.7**	**1.7**	**1.9**	**5.3**	**6.4**	**14.2**	**528**
Safety	22.3	17.8	4.2	5.1	24.6	.8	0.0	17.8	7.6	22.0	118
Fitness/ Mobility	23.3	70.7	8.9	0.0	3.3	.8	0.0	.8	2.4	13.0	123
Hazardous Environment	6.1	3.1	0.0	3.1	37.5	6.3	31.3	0.0	0.0	18.8	32
Deal with Public	2.8	6.7	0.0	40.0	13.3	0.0	0.0	0.0	26.7	13.3	15
Driving	7.8	24.4	0.0	2.4	17.1	2.4	0.0	12.2	2.4	39.0	41
Telephone	2.3	0.0	0.0	91.7	8.3	0.0	0.0	0.0	0.0	0.0	12
Paperwork	4.5	8.3	0.0	4.2	87.5	0.0	0.0	0.0	0.0	0.0	24
Stress	2.3	0.0	0.0	0.0	0.0	8.3	0.0	0.0	75.0	16.7	12
Manual Dexterity	6.3	63.6	6.1	0.0	18.2	6.1	0.0	3.0	0.0	3.0	33
Premises	18.8	50.5	46.5	0.0	1.0	1.0	0.0	0.0	0.0	1.0	99
Other	3.6	0.0	1.5	26.3	0.0	0.0	0.0	0.0	42.1	26.3	19

Population of Table (n) is all respondents indicating specific disabilities are a barrier to employment

Source: IMS Survey

6. Actions taken to Employ People with Disabilities

6.1 Introduction

Respondents to the postal survey were asked whether their organisation had undertaken any specific actions as a result of employing people with disabilities, in order to make it feasible or safe for them to do their job, or to improve their comfort or productivity.

6.2 Actions taken

Of the 1,104 respondents to this question, nearly a third (347 or 31.4 per cent) said that they had undertaken such specific actions, whilst 62 per cent had not, and seven per cent did not know.

Yet again it was size rather than sector which appeared to have the greatest influence on whether or not an employer had taken such actions, and the proportion who had taken actions increased strongly from a mere five per cent in the smallest size category, to over 90 per cent among organisations with 5,000 or more employees. This variation is to be expected since we have already seen that the likelihood of employing disabled people itself increases strongly with employment size.

More interesting, perhaps, is the proportion of those with employees with disabilities who had taken such actions. Of the 628 organisations with employees with disabilities who answered this question, 316 (or 50.3 per cent) had taken such actions. This suggests then, that despite the many obstacles and costs which employers without disabled employees typically anticipated in the recruitment and employment of people with disabilities, as many as a half of the employers who had employed disabled people had managed to do so, *without* the need to undertake any specific actions to accommodate them.

Concentrating only on those organisations that employ people with disabilities, we find the size effects becoming less marked. The proportion of the smallest organisations with disabled employees that have taken actions is one in five, a four-fold increase compared to all organisations with one to ten employees. However, among organisations with between 500 and 5,000 employees, the proportion of organisations with disabled employees that have taken actions is 55 per cent, an increase of only two percentage points compared with all organisations of this size.

The data suggest, furthermore, that employers with written policies relating to the employment of people with disabilities are more likely to have taken such actions than are those who have unwritten policies, who are in turn more likely to take actions than are those who have no policies (the relevant proportions are 66 per cent, 38 per cent and 13 per cent respectively). Several possible interpretations are possible here: one is that employers with formal policies are more likely than others to be aware of the kinds of action that may be required; alternatively it may be that employers with proactive, formal policies are more likely than others to recruit the kinds of disabled people for whom some accommodation is necessary (*eg* the more severely disabled).

Again, these differences become less marked when looking solely at organisations with disabled employees, so that the proportion of organisations with no policy that have taken action jumps from 13 per cent to 30 per cent, while for organisations with a written policy the rise is from 66 per cent to 73 per cent.

6.3 Actions taken for specific disabilities

Respondents who had undertaken specific actions were then asked to indicate the disabilities for which this had occurred and the nature of the action taken. Table 6.1 summarises the disabilities for which action had been taken (respondents used their own categorisation of disability, and these have subsequently been grouped for presentational purposes).

The largest single category of disabilities for which some kind of specific action had been taken is the broad group of disabilities affecting mobility or physical dexterity. Nearly three quarters of those employers who had taken some action had done so for this group. This is not unexpected given that the data in Chapter 2 showed that this category was the group of disabilities whose incidence was the greatest among employees in the sample. Similarly the second two most common categories of disability found in Chapter 2 (sensory difficulties) were the second two most common groups for whom actions were undertaken. For both seeing and hearing difficulties, just under a quarter of those taking action had done so for either or both of these groups of disabled employees.

It is striking from the Table that none of the other types of disability identified led to action by significant numbers of respondents. Even more striking, however, comparing the incidence of action taken for different categories of disability in Table 6.1, with the incidence of those disabilities in the sample of employers (see, for example, Table 2.5 above), that mobility and related disabilities have a higher tendency to require action on the part of the employer than any other types of disability. Thus Table 2.5 above showed that 78 per cent of the 633 respondents with disabled employees (*ie* 494 employers) had employees with mobility problems. Table 6.1, however, shows that 256 of these employers had taken action on behalf of employees with mobility problems; that is, employees with mobility–related disabilities had led to action in 52 per cent of these employers.

Table 6.1 Disabilities for which specific actions had been taken

Disability	% of all respondents taking action who had taken action for this disability
Mobility/dexterity: (incl. wheelchair)	73.7
Hearing difficulty	22.7
Seeing difficulty	22.5
Epilepsy	8.1
Mental handicap/learning difficulties	6.9
Chest/breathing problems	4.3
Heart/circulation problems	4.0
Diabetes	2.9
Depression/nerves/anxiety	1.7
Mental illness	1.7
Blood disorders	1.4
Restricted growth/dwarfism	1.4
Stomach/liver/kidneys/bladder/digestion	1.1
Allergy/skin condition	0.9
Drug/alcohol dependency	0.9
Speech impairment	0.6
Other/various/unspecified	23.1
TOTAL (N=)	347

Population of Table (n) is all respondents who have undertaken specific action to employ people with disabilities

Source: IMS Survey

The corresponding proportions for all other types of disability do not approach this figure: thus the proportion of employers with seeing disabilities in their workforces who had taken action is 40 per cent, for those with hearing disabilities the proportion is 26 per cent, and for those with mental handicap/severe learning difficulties it is 25 per cent. The disability with the next largest tendency to require action on the part of the employer is epilepsy; 12 per cent of employers with epileptic employees had taken such action. The figures for the other types of disability are even smaller.

These data do not, then, suggest an enormous burden on employers for most types of disability. Even mobility–related disabilities which tend to feature most strongly in the popular perception of disability, appear to require action by about only half of those employers who have such employees (interestingly only about a quarter of these mobility–related actions involved wheelchairs, the other main stereotype in this area). Other disabilities appear to be even less 'burdensome' in this respect[7].

Table 6.2 Main categories of specific action taken

Action	% of all respondents taking action who had taken the action in question
Provide special equipment	61.1
Modify premises	49.0
Reorganise work	22.8
Raise staff awareness	22.8
Special training	14.4
Monitor tasks/workload of individual	3.2
Provide special assistance	2.0
Provide clean environment	2.0
Flexible hours	1.7
Work from home	1.4
Counselling	1.2
Special foods provided	0.9
Involvement in disability forums	0.6
Not allow individual to work alone	0.3
Health insurance	0.3
Introduce extended health & safety policy for individuals	0.3
TOTAL (N =)	347

Population of Table (n) is all respondents who have undertaken specific actions to employ people with disabilities

Source: IMS Survey

Table 6.2 goes on to look at the main types of action which were taken, and as might be expected, given the main types of disabilities listed in the previous Table, the two largest categories were 'physical' actions, involving the provision of special equipment, or the modification of premises. Nearly all the other 'actions' frequently encountered, however, were organisational, involving modifications in the way things were done in the organisation.

---

[7]   Some caution is necessary here, however, since without more detailed information about recruitment practices it is not possible to be sure that there was not a tendency for employers to be more likely to recruit, among any category of disabled, those who were least likely to require any response or action on the part of the employer.

The relationships between the actions taken and the disabilities in question are shown in Table 6.3. Three quarters of organisations taking actions undertook them for people with mobility and sensory problems. Modifying premises was almost exclusively undertaken for people with mobility problems and those who are wheelchair bound, while around half of organisations providing special equipment and training did so for people with sensory impairments, and raising staff awareness was mainly undertaken for people with epilepsy.

Table 6.3 Actions taken by employers and disabilities in question

Problem	% of employers citing specific action, by disability									
	All	Mobility	Wheel-chair	Hearing	Seeing	Heart	Epilepsy	Mental Disorder	Other/ Various	N=
All	100.0	35.5	14.8	12.7	11.8	2.1	4.2	4.2	14.5	330
Provide equipment	38.8	36.7	4.7	21.9	25.8	0.8	0.8	0.0	9.4	128
Modify premises	31.8	50.5	39.0	1.0	0.0	0.0	0.0	0.0	9.5	105
Reorganise work	12.1	37.5	7.5	7.5	2.5	10.0	7.5	7.5	25.0	40
Provide training	4.5	0.0	0.0	26.7	26.7	6.7	0.0	26.7	13.3	15
Raise awareness	8.5	0.0	0.0	17.9	0.0	3.6	35.7	14.3	28.6	28
Other	4.2	14.3	7.1	7.1	7.1	0.0	0.0	21.4	42.9	14

Population of Table (n) is all respondents who have undertaken specific actions to employ people with disabilities

Source: IMS Survey

Examples of actions taken from case studies

The case study interviews generally reinforced the survey findings that mobility–related disabilities more frequently required actions to be taken and that these were often of a physical nature. Throughout the case studies numerous examples of these sorts of actions were given. They were not however, the only types of actions taken and there were many examples of other problems that had been very successfully overcome. Examples of these are considered below.

Mobility

On a very general level several organisations had specified that new office buildings must accommodate people with disabilities. A number of companies had moved to new but existing premises, but two organisations had recently had new office accommodation designed and built for them. A research and development group company stated that:

> '... when it was designed we ensured it incorporated all the main features necessary to cope with mobility problems. It was felt better to do it then, than have to spend money tacking it on later to cope with a new employee or an existing employee becoming disabled.'

More specific accommodations to cope with a particular individual's problems ranged from very minor alterations such as providing a special telephone for an employee with one hand who needed to be able to write or type whilst speaking on the phone, to developing customised or more complex specialist equipment. An electrical engineering company had a member of staff with a mobility problem so that she could not bend or twist to work around equipment she was assembling. The engineers at the company designed a work station which could support the equipment she was working on and tilt it into different positions to save her having to move around it.

There were also many examples of work being re–organised to take out physical aspects of a job which the individual could not undertake. A wholesale distribution company had several sales staff who had been found office based jobs either in management or telesales because they were no longer able to drive. Other examples included an MS sufferer working for a financial services organisation who had limited dexterity making some of the paperwork difficult. The job was redesigned to cover work she could do and tasks she could not were incorporated into other people's work areas.

Hearing difficulties

Hearing problems had also been successfully overcome by a number of organisations. Actions taken again ranged from reorganising the working environment to investing in special equipment.

An example of the former was in a wholesale distribution company where:

> 'We have a deaf woman who was employed to do desktop publishing. We arranged for her to work in an office with someone else so he can take her calls and look after her in fire drills. The ES originally paid part of her salary through the Job Introduction Scheme but we have now taken her on full time.'

Case Study 6.1 — Electronic Engineering Company

This company has a person who is profoundly deaf coming on work experience for six months. The preparation for this has involved quite a lot of work. The personnel manager has had to get a copy of all of the induction programme in writing for him to read first. She also then had to get the co–operation of the supervisor in the area where he was to work, who was, she admitted, sceptical at first. His parents have arranged to come in during half term to discuss any problems which they think may arise. When he starts he will be given a trainer to work with him on a one to one basis for two weeks, supported by a written training manual. They will use this as a test case to see if they could employ someone who is this deaf in the future. If he develops an aptitude to the work they will keep him on permanently.

The successful use of special equipment was illustrated by its introduction in the factory of a manufacturing company which had a number of deaf employees. The company introduced a mini–com system to aid deaf staff in the factory. This is like a telephone with a display and allows deaf employees in the factory to call other areas or floors. The welfare officer was learning sign language as well.

Seeing difficulty

People with visual impairment generally required specialist equipment to be supplied such as magnifying screens or document readers and some organisations with several blind staff had all company information and communications converted into braille. In some cases making suitable accommodations was not so straight-forward as *case study number 6.2* illustrates.

Case Study 6.2 — Local Authority

The council employed a blind WP operator so they installed speech back equipment which was partly government funded. They also provided training courses for her to learn how to use it. Accommodations were made for her guide dog and the section was arranged for ease of access. Alterations were made to the coding system for the work so that if dictation contained any tabular or indented work it is coded specifically. This work is then distributed to other WP operators. It ensures she does not receive work she can not do and avoids offending or upsetting her.

Epilepsy

Only one organisation interviewed had had to make any accommodations for an individual with epilepsy and these involved only minor re–organisations. A small manufacturing company had a woman who developed quite bad epilepsy during the time she was working for them. She still works in the same department but now has a first aider who works by her who is trained in the appropriate actions to take should she have a fit.

Diabetes

One company interviewed employed a diabetic who required no accommodations other than being allowed time off during working hours for his regular hospital treatment.

Restricted growth

When an electronic engineering company employed an individual with micromenia they faced a whole series of difficulties which were new to the personnel department despite already having a number of staff with disabilities. Their first project was to develop hand tools which were smaller than the usual equipment. He also needed a special chair which raised him up to the height of the work bench. When he started he was given a mentor to cover his training and induction. He went with him around the factory and work areas to discuss his special needs, for example whether he could reach the vending machine, whether the chairs in the coffee area were suitable *etc.* They wanted to sort this out before he started so the fuss could be minimal and would not make him feel different or uncomfortable.

General accommodations

Many companies made very general accommodations which were not intended for any particular individual but affected most existing staff and improved potential to employ new employees with disabilities. Examples of these include:

'The company has taken several general actions to encourage the employment of people with disabilities. We always try to be fairly flexible in individuals' working hours, content and location if possible to cover their various needs.' (Electronic engineering company)

'The personnel officer will hold discussions with staff in the group where disabled staff are recruited, especially with managers to help them avoid singling out an individual. They have regular team briefings which would cover issues involving a new disabled recruit.' (Electronic engineering company)

No accommodations

Several case study organisations indicated that despite having people with disabilities they had not found it necessary to make any accommodations and their disabilities did not affect their work in any way. The experience of this electrical engineering company was typical:

'We have three members of staff who have lost fingers from power press accidents. Although they could register as disabled it makes no difference to their working ability and no accommodations are necessary for them.'

6.4 Actions considered and rejected

A further indication of how 'difficult' employers found it to help or accommodate disabled employees was obtained by asking *all* survey respondents whether they had recently considered but rejected any of the kinds of actions discussed in the previous section. Of the 1,085 respondents who answered this question, only 17 (that is 1.6 per cent) said that they had considered and rejected such action.

Of these 17, six had considered and rejected a modification to premises, three had considered and rejected special training for disabled staff, three had considered and rejected disability awareness training for other staff, and two had considered and rejected a work reorganisation (the remaining ones did not specify the nature of the action rejected). Reasons given were to do with expense (six cases), practicality (four cases), a general unwillingness on the part of relevant staff or managers (two cases), and the fact that the buildings in question were listed and could not be modified (one case).

None of this suggests that respondents confronted with an apparent need for action to accommodate a disabled employee (or job applicant) were generally unable or unwilling to make that accommodation. It suggests rather the opposite.

6.5 Extra costs associated with disabled employees

A key issue which typically arises in any discussion of employers' attitudes towards the employment of people with disabilities, concerns the question of how much extra (if any) it costs for an employer to employ people with disabilities. Many of the anxieties of employers who do not employ people with disabilities (discussed, for example, in Chapter 3 above) implicitly stem from concerns about cost (whether directly through special equipment, building adaptation *etc.*, or indirectly through lower productivity, less efficient work schedules, managerial and supervisory time *etc.*).

All respondents to the postal survey were asked, therefore, whether there were in fact (or whether they thought there would be) any extra costs to the organisation associated with recruiting or employing people with disabilities.

Of the 1,077 who answered this question, 466 (or 43 per cent) thought there would be extra costs, 24 per cent did not, and 32.3 per cent did not know. There was no obvious systematic or sectoral pattern to this response, but interestingly, the belief that extra costs would be involved appeared to increase somewhat with organisational size — from 31 per cent in the smallest size category (ten or fewer employees), to 64 per cent in the largest category (5,000 or more employees). At one level this seems slightly counter–intuitive, since one might expect the smallest firms to have the greatest anxiety about the extra cost burdens that employing people with disabilities might impose. Alternatively, however, it is possible that smaller firms, because of their greater informality and flexibility, and perhaps lower levels of technology and organisational complexity, are more likely to be able to accommodate disabled employees without significant cost implications. We should of course remember from previous chapters that the largest firms are much more likely to have employees with disabilities, and this finding might therefore be explained in terms of their experience of employing people with disabilities which made them aware of the costs involved. The data do not support such an explanation, however; there is little difference between the proportion of organisations with disabled employees who believe that extra costs are involved (46 per cent), and the corresponding proportion of organisations without disabled employees (40 per cent), and the difference is not statistically significant.

The next question to ask, of course, is *how much* extra cost the organisation would be prepared to incur as a result of recruiting a person with disabilities. In asking this question, the questionnaire tried to take account firstly of the possibility that the level within the organisation to which the disabled employee was being recruited would affect the amount the employer was willing to pay (the question was therefore asked in terms of three hypothetical employees — at gross equivalent annual salaries of eight, fifteen and twenty two thousand pounds). Secondly, the questioning attempted to take account of extra costs which were initial, 'one off' costs associated with employing people with disabilities (building adaptations, special equipment, for example), and ongoing recurrent costs (associated with lower productivity, supervisory costs *etc.*). For details of the questions used, see the questionnaire in Appendix 2.

In practice only a minority of respondents (between 167 and 212) answered this set of questions, suggesting *either* that employers do not tend to think this way, in terms of upper limits to their extra expenditure associated with disabled employees, *or* that the question was badly designed. In practice, the comments written by non–respondents on the questionnaire, and information provided by case study respondents on this issue suggest the former rather than the latter. The case studies in particular indicated that almost without exception respondents could not put a top limit, in abstract, on their expenditure, arguing that 'it would depend on the individual case', although several stressed that this certainly did not mean that they would be prepared to spend an unlimited amount (the word 'reasonable' cropped up often in this context), and a few suggested that any limit might be in terms of the total amount the organisation would be prepared to spend overall on being 'disability friendly', rather than there being a limit for any particular person (much expenditure, particularly physical accommodations, for example, can benefit several or many disabled employees).

Turning briefly to the case studies, the following are typical of the comments made during the case study interviews which further expand on the points raised on costs in the survey:

> 'Costs are obviously important and if alterations are very expensive numerous factors have to be taken into account. What is questioned is for example, whether anyone else, staff and customers, will benefit from this; how long is the lease on the building; is it worth making alterations to this building if the lease expires? In such circumstances business conditions are of paramount importance.' (Transport and communications company)

> 'Cost is obviously an important element. At the end of the day we are here to run a business. You can not really estimate the cost in accommodating these people because it's mainly time spent by myself in re–organising things.' (Financial services company)

> 'Financial considerations are not what it is all about. The limit is not on what you spend, it is the management time. How many people can you afford to handle. Supervisors don't really have the time and senior management time may be available but is at a premium.' (Electrical engineering company)

> 'The main cost is the time spent. For physical alterations there are always grants available. It's not really down to money, it is about being prepared to put in time.' (Electronic engineering company)

> 'I put down on the questionnaire that we would spend £1,000 initially and £4,000 ongoing cost per year. These amounts are not significant to us now. If it was any more we would have to think

about it but £4,000 is not much out of the overall cost of 260 employees. Really you need £1,000 to modify a machine for a disabled person and £1,000 of time to supervise them.' (Electrical engineering company)

'Overall we would not turn anything down because of lack of funds, within reason.' (Financial services company)

We have set out in Table 6.4 the average costs which employers stated they would be prepared to spend as result of recruiting a person with a disability.

Table 6.4 Maximum acceptable extra cost associated with employing a person

Gross equivalent annual salary of post to which person is recruited (£ p.a.)	Average maximum initial cost respondents would be prepared to pay (£)	Average maximum ongoing cost respondents would be prepared to pay (£ p.a.)
NB: No. of respondents in brackets		
£8,000	£795.14 (197)	£549.66 (212)
£15,000	£1,029.85 (174)	£631.47 (185)
£22,000	£1,169.13 (167)	£817.88 (177)

Population of Table (n) is all respondents answering question on cost

Source: IMS Survey

The data confirm that insofar as there are limits to the extra acceptable costs, the limits increase with the salary of the employee concerned, but not in proportion to the increase in salary. Thus respondents would be prepared to pay up to between five per cent (for a higher paid employee) and ten per cent (for a lower paid one) of gross annual salary, in initial costs of accommodating an employee with a disability. As far as ongoing costs are concerned, the corresponding range is between four and seven per cent of gross salary cost per year. It is interesting to note in this context (see the literature review in Appendix 3), that insofar as there are any estimates of how much actual accommodations for disabled employees cost, they tend to be rather lower on average than these figures.

Finally, respondents were asked whether they would be prepared to spend more than these limits if the person in question was an existing employee. Of the 901 respondents to this question, 39 per cent said they would be prepared to spend more, 14 per cent said they would not be, and 48 per cent did not know. Further analysis suggested that the proportion prepared to spend more on existing employees increased strongly with size (25 per cent in the smallest size group, 68 per cent in the largest), whilst the proportion prepared to spend more was higher (at 49 per cent) among those who currently employed people with disabilities, than among those who did not (25 per cent). This is consistent with the notion that the larger organisations, who are more likely to have employees with disabilities, are also more likely to have experienced an existing employee becoming disabled, and understand the greater pressure to 'do the right thing' which such cases generate.

Looking at the case study interviews, views varied with respect to the difference in amounts an organisation would spend on an existing employee compared with that spent on a new recruit. Some admitted that they would do more for existing employees because they felt they were investing in someone who was already known to the company as a valued employee:

> 'If they were valued we would do more.'

One respondent also reluctantly admitted that what they would do would very much depend on the level of responsibility of the member of staff. If it was a junior clerk, they would be much less likely even to consider costly changes than if it was a member of the management team.

On the other hand one personnel officer from an electronics company did believe that there should be no difference. She said it was very difficult to put a financial limit on what they would be prepared to do. She answered the questionnaire in terms of a £1,000 initial outlay which would cover cost of such things as a special chair *etc*. It was really a figure 'off the top of her head', and she also quoted £250 p.a. on an ongoing, which was really to cover management time *etc*. She did not feel that the level of the member of staff or whether they were a new recruit would make any difference to the amount spent.

7. Use of External Help, Support and Advice

7.1 Introduction

An important part of the study involved an examination of employers' perceptions and use of external support and advice (including that supplied through government agencies such as the Employment Service) relating to the employment of people with disabilities. Respondents to the postal survey were asked, therefore, whether they had sought any such external support or advice, and if so, from whom they had sought it and what kind of support/advice they had sought. They were also asked whether they had received the help they required, and to indicate whether there were any forms of external support which they had not received, but would find helpful in this context.

7.2 Who seeks external support and advice?

Of the 1,093 respondents answering these questions, fewer than a third (338 or 31 per cent) claimed to have sought external help, support or advice with regard to the recruitment or employment of people with disabilities, whilst nearly two thirds (665 or 61 per cent) had not done so, and a further 90 (eight per cent) did not know whether their organisation had sought such support or advice.

Given the long standing existence of provision of such support and advice (particularly through the Employment Service and the voluntary sector), coupled with the perceived difficulties of many employers in recruiting and employing people with disabilities which we have seen in earlier chapters, and their widespread failure to meet their legal obligations in terms of the three per cent quota, it is perhaps surprising that such a small proportion apparently feel the need to look outside for guidance and support. More interesting, however, is the question of which kinds of organisation look for such advice and support and which ones do not.

Table 7.1 looks at how this propensity to seek outside advice and support varies by sector and size of organisation. There are clear and significant sectoral variations — generally speaking, organisations in parts of manufacturing and energy and water supply sectors are most likely to have sought such advice/support (notably energy and water supply and metals and minerals). The rest of manufacturing (engineering and other manufacturing) together with parts of the service sector (financial and business services and other services) all have lower and fairly similar tendencies to look outside for external support (around a third of respondents in each case). The propensity is slightly lower in distribution and hotels, lower still in transport and communications, and lowest of all in the construction sector.

Again, however, given the large differences in the size composition of different sectors, the suspicion remains that many of these differences are essentially picking up a size effect. Table 7.1 confirms that there is such an effect, and that it is strong and highly significant; there is a steadily increasing tendency with increasing employment size to use outside support and advice in connection with the recruitment/employment of people with disabilities. This varies from one in forty of the smallest organisations having sought such support, to nearly ninety per cent of the largest employers having done so.

Table 7.1 Use of external advice/support by size and sector

| | % | | | |
	Yes	No	Don't Know	N=
Total	**30.9**	**60.8**	**8.2**	**1,093**
Sector				
Energy/Water supply	70.4	18.5	11.1	27
Metals/Minerals	43.4	43.4	13.2	76
Engineering	29.2	62.7	8.1	209
Other Manufacturing	36.1	56.9	6.9	72
Construction	8.3	88.9	2.8	72
Distribution/Hotels	27.3	64.8	8.0	176
Transport/Communication	17.6	70.4	12.0	108
Financial and Business Services	35.1	60.8	4.1	194
Other Services	36.7	51.9	11.4	158
Number of employees				
1 – 10	2.5	91.4	6.1	198
11 – 49	10.6	78.9	10.6	199
50 – 199	27.6	65.2	7.2	221
200 – 499	38.4	53.5	8.1	185
500 – 4999	56.6	32.7	10.7	159
5000+	87.0	7.6	5.4	86

Population of Table (n) is all respondents in sample

Note: Sector SIC 0 Agriculture, Forestry and Fishing was not included — see Appendix 1, Section 1.2

Source: IMS Survey

This is a pattern familiar from research looking at more general sources of business and employment advice and support provision to small and medium–sized enterprises (see, for example, Atkinson and Meager 1993). That is, the organisations apparently most in need of such advice and support, and whose management and organisational practices could most benefit from it (namely the smallest firms), are the ones least likely to be aware of its existence, least likely to recognise a need for it, and least likely to seek it out. Similarly we have seen in previous chapters that smaller organisations are, generally speaking, less likely to recruit and employ people with disabilities, and most likely to perceive problems and difficulties in so doing. *A priori*, therefore, they would appear to have the greatest potential benefit to derive from external support and advice provision.

Yet again, however, we must be careful in not drawing over–strong conclusions from this. There are several possible motivations for an organisation in wishing to seek such support/advice. In particular, it is worth distinguishing between:

i   organisations who do not employ people with disabilities, but who: wish to, feel that they ought to do so, or who wish to find ways of overcoming the barriers they perceive to do doing so;

ii organisations who already have employees with disabilities, who receive applications from such people, or who have existing employees who have become disabled, and who therefore wish to find ways of making provision or accommodation for them.

Chapter 3 showed that the dominant reason for not employing people with disabilities (particularly among smaller firms) is that none have applied to the firm for employment. Arguably, therefore, case (i) above is the less plausible of the two for seeking external support and advice, the trigger for which is more likely to be applications for employment from disabled people or an existing employee becoming disabled. We have already argued that larger firms are more likely, simply by virtue of their size and the greater volume of their recruitment activity, to encounter disabled applicants or employees, and hence the perceived need for external support and advice is more likely to be triggered than in a smaller firm.[8] This interpretation was supported by much of the evidence from the smaller case study organisations, who often took the line '... we would seek such support only as and when we need it; for example, if one of our employees became disabled'.

There may be some important policy implications here. The understanding that there is some obligation (for all but the smallest firms) to employ disabled people, that there may also be considerable

---

[8]   We have also noted in previous chapters that smaller firms are less likely than large ones to have proactive policies on the recruitment and employment of people with disabilities. Again some care needs to be taken in interpreting causality here — large firms are more likely to encounter disabled people in employment or applying for jobs, and this experience may itself be the motivation to develop a policy (rather than *vice versa*).

Institute of Manpower Studies

benefits to the firm in doing so, and that 'good practice' implies a positive and proactive stance, is a message that has not reached many small organisations. Such organisations are unlikely to recognise the need for such advice and to seek it out. Therefore, unless prompted by force of circumstance. Marketing of existing support and provision to such smaller organisations is therefore important (perhaps through the means of other intermediary bodies who are in regular contact with small businesses — TECs are likely to have an increasingly important role here). It is also worth noting in this context that some of the case study responses suggested that even where there was an awareness of advice and support available through the Employment Service, for example, it was often believed that such provision was appropriate only for dealing with a specific issue and a specific disability, rather than for providing more general advice about good practice in recruitment, employment, training *etc*.

More support for the argument that it is the organisations who already have employees with disabilities, and who already take a positive, proactive stance in this area, who are most likely to seek external support and advice, is provided in Table 7.2.

Table 7.2 Use of external advice/support, by existing employment of, and policy

	% of respondents having sought external advice/support	Total (N =)
Whether currently employ people with disabilities		
Yes	48.4	626
No	7.7	444
Don't know	5.0	20
Whether have formal policy on employing people with disabilities		
Yes, written	66.1	280
Yes, unwritten	37.0	208
No	13.0	568
Don't know	3.6	28

Population of Table (n) is all respondents in sample

Source: IMS Survey

7.3 Sources of external advice and support

To whom then did our respondents turn for advice and support in recruiting and employing people with disabilities? Table 7.3 shows, firstly, that among the third or so of respondents who did seek such advice and support, the main Employment Department organisations effectively dominate the market, with nearly 80 per cent of this group using the various ES services (DRO/DAS/PACT), and nearly half using the Jobcentre. By comparison, the other sources were used infrequently, with the Local Authority, the local TEC and the Citizens' Advice Bureau being used by some 16 per cent, 13 per cent and three per cent of this group respectively. 'Other' sources of advice and support were listed by 17 per cent of respondents, and these were, for the most part, the various voluntary organisations and charities dealing with disability issues, or local networks of such bodies.

Table 7.3 Source of help, support etc.

Source	% using the source	Nature of assistance received (% of users of each source. Note: can total more than 100%)			
		Practical/ financial	Advice/ information	Referral to other sources	Total users of source
DRO/DAS/ PACT	79.0	49.1	95.1	27.7	267
Jobcentre	47.3	31.9	86.9	20.0	160
TEC	12.7	41.9	83.7	32.6	43
Local Authority	16.3	40.0	89.1	18.2	55
Citizens' Advice Bureau	3.3	18.2	100.0	9.1	11
Other	16.9	40.4	93.0	35.1	57

Total users of advice (N=) 338

Population of Table (n) is all respondents having sought external advice/support

Source: IMS Survey

The Table also looks at what kind of assistance employers actually received from these different organisations (*ie* whether it was mainly practical/financial help, whether it involved advice or information, or whether the organisation referred the employer on to other sources of assistance). It can be seen firstly that the main form of assistance provided by all the sources was advice and information (in each case over 80 per cent of those seeking assistance got this). In nearly all the cases the source provided practical or financial help about half as often as it provided advice and information (the sole exception being the CABs which provided advice/information in all cases, and practical or financial help relatively rarely — as would be expected, given the nature of these organisations). The various sources differed rather more in the extent to which they referred the employer on to other sources of assistance — TECs, in particular, were the most likely to do this.

It is also of some interest, given the significant variation in the propensity to seek assistance between different organisations (especially between different employment size bands) noted above, to ask whether the penetration of the various advice and support organisations varied between different parts of the employer market. Table 7.4 looks at this question.

Table 7.4 Use of different advice/support sources

| | % using source | | | | | | |
	DRO/ DAS /PACT	Job-centre	TEC	Local Auth.	CAB	Other	Total (N=)
Total	**79.0**	**47.3**	**12.7**	**16.3**	**3.3**	**16.9**	**338**
Sector							
Energy/Water supply	89.4	47.4	21.1	36.8	0.0	26.3	19
Metals/Minerals	81.8	54.5	9.1	12.1	3.0	12.1	33
Engineering	78.7	57.4	4.9	16.4	0.0	11.5	61
Other Manufacturing	80.8	53.8	7.7	3.8	0.0	11.5	26
Construction	100.0	66.7	16.7	0.0	0.0	0.0	6
Distribution/Hotels	58.3	39.6	14.6	18.8	8.3	18.8	48
Transport/Comm	68.4	47.4	21.1	15.8	0.0	26.3	19
Financial/Bus. Services	85.3	42.6	13.2	19.1	4.4	23.5	68
Other Services	84.5	39.7	17.2	13.8	5.2	13.8	58
Number of employees							
1 – 10	60.0	40.0	40.0	20.0	0.0	20.0	5
11 – 49	61.9	47.6	9.5	19.0	9.5	9.5	21
50 – 199	73.8	36.1	11.5	16.4	3.3	8.2	61
200 – 499	67.6	50.7	5.6	14.1	0.0	8.5	71
500 – 4999	86.7	55.6	13.3	11.1	3.3	18.9	90
5000+	92.5	47.5	18.8	20.0	5.0	28.8	80

Population of Table (n) is all respondents having sought external advice/support

Note: Sector SIC 0 Agriculture, Forestry and Fishing was not included — see Appendix 1, Section 1.2

Source: IMS Survey

As far as sector is concerned, there are variations between the different advice sources used by the employers in different sectors, but they do not fall into any clear pattern, and they are not, for the most part, statistically significant.

The variation by size is more interesting, since although there is a general tendency for the use of all advice/support sources to increase with employment size, this increase is most consistent and marked for the use of the Employment Service (DRO/DAS/PACT). Thus although the Employment Service has the greatest share of this 'market' for all size groups, its relative advantage is far greater in the larger size groups. Thus, as might be expected, some of the less 'specialist' advice sources achieve relatively higher penetration in the smaller size groups. It is notable, for example, that the use of the Jobcentre for such purposes varies relatively little with size, and this variation is statistically insignificant. Similarly, the TEC and the Local Authority appear to do relatively 'well' in the smaller size categories, although small numbers in some cells urge caution here.

Whilst these findings are somewhat short of conclusive, they reinforce the notion that the smaller organisations are ill–served by most of the existing sources. Some of the 'generalist' agencies are relatively more successful among these employer groups, and the successful marketing of more specialist disability services to the smallest employers could perhaps most effectively occur through referral networks with such other agencies.

Finally, it is also of some interest to consider whether employers who already have employees with disabilities tend to use different advice sources than those who do not; that is, are there any advice sources which are relatively more successful than others in getting to the group of employers who do not employ people with disabilities?

Table 7.5 Use of different advice/support sources by current employment of people

| | % using source | | | | | | |
	DRO/DAS /PACT	Job- centre	TEC	Local Auth.	CAB	Other	Total (N=)
Total	79.0	47.3	12.7	16.3	3.3	16.9	338
Employ people with disabilities?							
Yes	81.8	47.5	13.5	15.8	3.6	17.8	303
No	52.9	47.1	5.9	20.6	0.0	8.8	34
Don't know	0.0	0.0	0.0	0.0	0.0	0.0	1

Population of Table (n) is all respondents having sought external advice/support

Source: IMS Survey

Again, given the small number of respondents who do not employ people with disabilities who have sought any form of support/advice, Table 7.5 does not permit strong conclusions; and again it is clear that the Employment Service provision dominates the sources among both those who do and those who do not employ people with disabilities. Yet again, however, it would seem that the Employment Service's relative advantage (over generalist sources of advice such as the Jobcentre and the Local Authority) is much smaller among employers who do not employ people with disabilities, than it is among those who do. This is again consistent with some of the case study evidence that the offerings of the Employment Service are seen more as a source of disability–specific advice for employers who already do (or who have decided to employ) someone with a disability, rather than a source of general information and advocacy on the benefits of employing people with a disability, and how to go about attracting and recruiting such people.

7.4 Failed attempts to obtain advice/support

Respondents were also asked to indicate whether they had sought but failed to get advice/support relating to the recruitment/employment of people with disabilities, from any of the above agencies. Table 7.6 reports their responses, and calculates 'dissatisfaction rates', *ie* those who were unsuccessful in obtaining advice/support from a given organisation as a percentage of all those who sought advice from that organisation (successfully or unsuccessfully).

Table 7.6 'Dissatisfaction rates' by source of advice/support

Source of advice/support	% of those seeking advice/support who did not get it	Total seeking advice/support (N=)
DRO/DAS/PACT	5.7	283
Jobcentre	6.4	171
TEC	6.5	46
Local authority	8.3	60
CAB	15.4	13
Other	5.0	60

Population of Table (n) is all respondents having sought but failed to get advice/support

Source: IMS Survey

The key feature which stands out from the Table is how low the dissatisfaction rate for all the different types of agencies is; in all cases bar one it lies well below ten per cent (and the slightly higher rate recorded for the Citizens' Advice Bureau cannot be given much weight given the very small numbers involved).

Taking these findings together with those in previous sections, therefore, they suggest that the range of advice and support currently available to employers is generally adequate, in the sense that those employers who sought assistance or support from these organisations nearly always got it. The main deficiency in this area, rather, would seem to be that there are large numbers of employers, particularly the smallest employers and those who do not currently employ people with disabilities, who tend not to seek advice and support. To reach these organisations (which clearly need to be reached, if the overall level of employment of people with disabilities is to be increased significantly), a greater emphasis on active marketing and 'outreach' work might therefore be required.

7.5 More help needed?

Finally, in order to gauge the extent and nature of unmet employer need in this area, respondents were asked whether there was any form of help, support or advice from government or other agencies which they would find particularly helpful in the recruitment or employment of people with disabilities.

Only a small minority of the 1,043 respondents answering this question (some 16 per cent) said that there was some additional assistance which they would find helpful in this regard, a further 44 per cent stated that there was not, whilst 40 per cent did not have an opinion on this.

Table 7.7 shows how this varies by sector and by size — there is some sectoral variation, but it does not fall into any strong or clear pattern, with the largest proportions looking for more assistance found in energy and water supply, financial and business and other services. These latter sectors are, however, ones with a size structure containing a higher than average proportion of large firms, and the Table also confirms a strong and significant relationship with size. The largest organisations are eight times more likely than the smallest to think that additional external advice or support would be helpful, further reinforcing the notion put forward above, that not only are small firms less likely than average to use such services, but they are also less likely than average to recognise or articulate a need for them.

Finally, respondents indicating a wish for more or different external assistance from government or other agencies, were asked to indicate what would be most useful in this area. The question was an 'open–ended' one and respondents suggestions have been grouped into broad categories and summarised in Table 7.8.

It is perhaps unsurprising that the largest single category of greater assistance required was financial — over a third of those giving suggestions suggested that the government should invest more (through larger payments, and/or wider eligibility than currently

Table 7.7 Requirements for additional advice/support by size and sector

	Yes	No	Don't know	N=
Total	**16.0**	**44.3**	**39.7**	**1,043**
Sector				
Energy/Water supply	29.6	40.7	29.6	27
Metals/Minerals	14.1	52.1	33.8	71
Engineering	11.4	47.8	40.8	201
Other Manufacturing	12.1	50.0	37.9	66
Construction	12.9	44.3	42.9	70
Distribution/Hotels	14.5	42.4	43.0	165
Transport/Communication	10.4	47.2	42.5	106
Financial/Business Services	21.5	44.6	33.9	186
Other Services	22.7	34.0	43.3	150
Number of employees				
1 – 10	5.8	48.2	46.1	191
11 – 49	9.2	44.1	46.7	195
50 – 199	16.4	45.8	37.9	214
200 – 499	15.9	44.3	39.8	176
500 – 4999	24.1	38.6	37.2	145
5000+	44.0	33.3	22.6	84

Population of Table (n) is all respondents indicating requirement for additional advice/support

Note: Sector SIC 0 Agriculture, Forestry and Fishing was not included — see Appendix 1, Section 1.2

Source: IMS Survey

---

exists for government funded support for employing people with disabilities) in grants to enable/encourage employers to recruit and retain people with disabilities. Suggestions covered both wage subsidies (in which context a further four per cent of these respondents advocated an expansion of the Sheltered Placement Scheme), and financial aid for specific purposes such as equipment purchase, buildings modification *etc.*

Some suggestions related to changes in the operation or emphasis of existing services — *eg* a system of back–up visits from DROs (20 per cent), a more proactive stance from the PACT teams (nine per cent).

Table 7.8 Extra categories of external assistance required

Form of assistance	% citing category
Financial grants	37.8
Back–up visits from the DRO	20.1
Directories of disability agencies/charities dealing with recruitment	16.5
Co–ordination between government depts. in information/support to employers	12.2
PACTs to be proactive in liaising between employers and disabled	9.1
More/better advice on use and availability of special equipment	8.5
Publicity for disabled role models	7.9
Anti–discrimination legislation in the disability area	6.7
Revised definition of disability	4.3
Training programmes for people with disabilities	3.7
Expansion of Sheltered Placement Scheme	3.7
Enforcement of quota	3.0
Funding for/provision of disability awareness training	3.0
Medical assessments	1.2
Abolition of quota system	1.2
Relax Income Support criteria for disabled people working part–time	1.2
Transport assistance	0.6
Obligation on disabled people to report part–time work requirement for additional advice/support	0.6
Marketing of ES disability symbol to people with disabilities	0.6
TOTAL (N=)	164

Population of Table (n) is all respondents indicating a requirement for additional advice/support

Source: IMS Survey

Others essentially saw public bodies playing a more effective co–ordinating/facilitating role, for example, through publication of directories of voluntary sector and charitable training providers and other potential sources of disabled labour (17 per cent), or through improving the co–ordination of public agencies and their relationships with networks of employers (12 per cent). In this context it is interesting that some of the case study respondents argued strongly that a major problem for employers in wishing to recruit actively from people with disabilities is one of accessing the pool of inactive/unemployed disabled labour — they would wish to deal with the voluntary sector as a potential source of such supply, but find it fragmented, ill–co–ordinated and competitive. One such respondent said:

> '... we'd be keen to do more, but when we think we've got vacancies that would be suitable for disabled people, we try and contact some of the charities, but they hardly ever come up with anyone, and they don't seem to pass the word around among themselves... perhaps this is something the TEC could do.'

Some respondents (generally the 'better practice' ones) did also mention membership of various employer networks (such as the Employers' Forum on Disability, and some local/regional equivalents) as a useful mechanism here.

On the legislative front, it is interesting that only two respondents argued for abolition of the three per cent quota (as against five who argued that it should be enforced); whilst seven per cent argued for the introduction of anti–discrimination legislation for people with disabilities.

APPENDICES

Contents to Appendices

Appendix 1
Research Methods and
Sample Characteristics

1 Research Methods and Sample Characteristics

1.1 Introduction

In this Appendix we consider the research methodology, and then go on to describe the characteristics of the achieved sample, on which the results discussed in the previous chapters are based.

1.2 Research methods and target sample characteristics

The research was conducted using a self–completion postal questionnaire, agreed in discussion with the Employment Department. A copy of the questionnaire is shown in Appendix 2. This was followed up by more detailed case–study interviews with a small number of respondents.

The total sample comprised of two sub–samples, both of which were drawn at organisation level rather than establishment level, as we were mainly interested in the overall policy and practice issues throughout the whole organisation, rather than the actual practice in individual establishments. The first sub–sample was a random sample and was drawn from Dun and Bradstreet, chosen because it is an organisation–based database. The second was a control sample of employers known or believed to recruit and employ people with disabilities, and to exhibit 'good practice' as regards the employment of people with disabilities. This smaller sub–sample was chosen from lists of employers who used the Employment Service disability symbol, or who were involved with the Employers' Forum on Disabilities or Opportunities for Disabled. The questionnaire for the random sample was addressed to 'The Personnel Director', while the questionnaire for the 'good practice' sample was personally addressed to the person responsible for equal opportunities within the organisation. In both cases two full reminders were sent to non–respondents.

The random sample aimed at broad representativeness, and was structured by employment size and by industrial sector, as shown in Table 1.1. Sector SIC 0 Agriculture, Forestry and Fishing was excluded from the survey due to the preponderance of very small employers in this sector and the difficulty of constructing a reliable employer based sample frame in the time available for the survey. Given however, that this sector accounts for a mere 1.4 per cent of UK employees (Census of Employment 1991) it was not believed that this exclusion detracts from the reliability of the survey. However, as the control sample was aimed at 'good practice' employers, it was not

Table 1.1 Structure of initial random sample

SIC Code	Number of Employees			
	< 100	**100–199**	**200+**	**Total**
1–4	134	71	246	451
5	91	12	22	125
6–9	847	165	408	1,420
Total	1,072	248	676	1,996

Source: IMS Survey

meant to be representative in terms of size and structure, and the sample characteristics were not recorded.

The response rates for the total sample and the two sub–samples are summarised in Table 1.2. The initial mailing of 2,308 questionnaires consisted of 1,996 in the random sub–sample and 312 in the 'good practice' sub–sample. After eliminating the Post Office Returns and questionnaires addressed to inappropriate organisations[9] the effective samples were 2,156, 1,855, and 301 respectively for the total sample and the random and control sub–samples.

There were 1,123 useable replies to the survey as a whole, giving an overall response rate of 49 per cent and an effective response rate of 52 per cent. The corresponding response rates for the random sub–sample were 46 per cent and 50 per cent, and for the control sub–sample were 64 per cent and 66 per cent.

Table 1.2 Survey response summary

	Total sample	Random sub-sample	Control sub-sample
Initial Mailing	2,308	1,996	312
Post Office Returns *etc.*	152	141	11
Effective Sample	2,156	1,855	301
Total Returns	1,151	-	-
Not Completed	28	-	-
Participants	1,123	924	199
	%	%	%
Overall Response Rate	48.7	46.3	63.8
Effective Response Rate	52.1	49.8	66.1

Source: IMS Survey

---

[9] *Eg* these were organisations which turned out not to be 'employers' in the required sense, such as some voluntary and religious organisations, or self–employed sole traders.

Institute of Manpower Studies

Because the random sub–sample was structured by employment size and industrial sector, we were able to calculate response rates for the individual size and sector categories to see if they was any response bias to the sample. Table 1.3 shows the effective sample (*ie* after eliminating the Post Office Returns, *etc.*), broken down by employment size and sector, and Table 1.4 shows the response rates for each size and sector category of the random sample. There is very little variation in the response rates between the different sectors and size bands, so we can be fairly confident that there was no significant and systematic bias, by size or by sector, in the responses to the random sub–sample.[10]

Table 1.3 Structure of effective random sample

SIC Code	Number of Employees			
	< 100	100–199	200+	Total
1–4	124	68	245	437
5	82	12	22	116
6–9	744	159	399	1,302
Total	950	239	666	1,855

Source: IMS Survey

Table 1.4 Response rates for the random sample by size and sector (%)

SIC Code	Number of Employees			
	< 100	100–199	200+	Total
1–4	55.6	44.1	53.1	52.4
5	53.7	25.0	45.5	49.1
6–9	47.7	56.0	48.6	49.0
Total	49.3	51.0	50.2	49.8

Source: IMS Survey

[10] It should be noted that these response rates refer to numbers of questionnaires received from each size and sector category, rather than the responses given to the questions on industrial sector and numbers of employees. Among the responses there was a bias towards smaller organisations and the production sector, which may be accounted for by questionnaires being answered by a single establishment or other unit whose employment size and main activity is different to that of the organisation as a whole, and by employers reducing employment levels during the recession.

As mentioned above, a selection of respondents to the postal survey was chosen for detailed interviews to flesh out the questionnaire responses. The respondents were chosen on the basis of both their structural characteristics and their responses to the survey, to get a reasonable split between those employing/not employing people with disabilities and those 'positive'/'negative' attitudes towards employing disabled people, as well as to achieve a reasonable spread of sizes and sectors.

Twenty one such case–studies were undertaken, and the characteristics of those organisations that were interviewed is shown in Table 1.5.

Table 1.5 Characteristics of case–study organisations

	No. of Organisations
Employing people with disabilities	15
Not employing people with disabilities	6
SIC 1–4	6
SIC 5	1
SIC 6–9	14
<100 Employees	5
100–199 Employees	2
200+ Employees	14
'Good practice' employers	8
Organisations from random sub–sample	13

Source: IMS Survey

1.3 Characteristics of the achieved sample

Respondents were asked to provide the following background information about their organisation or establishment: whether they were answering on behalf of the whole organisation, a single establishment, or some other unit; whether they were in the private sector, the public sector, or the voluntary sector; the main activity of the organisation/establishment; and the number of employees at the organisation/establishment.

Table 1.6 presents the background characteristics of the total achieved sample and the two sub–samples. Examining first on whose behalf the questions were answered, 75 per cent of respondents answered on behalf of the whole organisation, 21 per cent answered on behalf of a single site or establishment, while four per cent of answers were on behalf of some other unit, such as a divisional or regional office. There was very little variation in these proportions between the random sample and the 'good practice' sample.

Table 1.6 Background information on the achieved sample

		Total Sample (%)	Random Sub–sample (%)	Control Sub–sample (%)
Responses on behalf of:				
Whole Organisation		74.8	74.9	74.1
Single Establishment		21.2	21.5	19.8
Other Unit		4.0	3.5	6.1
	N=	1107	910	197
Ownership				
Private Sector		93.0	96.0	79.3
Public Sector		5.8	3.1	18.7
Voluntary Sector		1.2	1.0	2.0
	N=	1113	915	198
Industrial Sector				
Energy/Water Supply		2.4	1.5	7.0
Metals/Minerals		7.0	6.5	9.0
Engineering		19.1	21.1	9.5
Other Manufacturing		6.4	5.9	9.0
Construction		6.5	7.3	3.0
Distribution/Hotels/Catering		16.0	17.4	9.5
Transport/Communication		10.2	11.1	5.5
Business Services		17.9	16.5	24.6
Other Services		14.5	12.8	22.6
	N=	1122	923	199
Number of Employees				
1–10		19.6	23.6	1.0
11–49		19.2	22.2	5.2
50–199		20.7	21.3	17.7
200–499		17.3	19.2	8.9
500–4999		14.7	12.0	27.6
5000+		8.5	1.8	39.6
	N=	1079	887	192

Source: IMS Survey

Just over nine out of ten of all respondents were in the private sector, while six per cent were in the public sector and one per cent in the voluntary sector. However, among the 'good practice' sample, over one in five respondents were in the public and voluntary sectors, and among the random sample fewer than one in twenty were in either the public or the voluntary sector.

Around a third of respondents were in the production industries (SIC 1–4), seven per cent were in construction, and around 60 per cent are in the service industries (SIC 6–9). These proportions vary little between the random sample and the 'good practice' sample, although there is rather more variation when looking at the individual industries. In particular, engineering, construction, and distribution, hotels and catering are over–represented in the random sample, while energy and water supply, financial and business services, and other services are over–represented in the control sample. Turning to the size distribution, we find that small and medium sized organisations are concentrated in the random sample, and that the largest organisations are mainly to be found in the 'good practice' sample.

Finally, Table 1.7 shows the breakdown of size of establishment by sector for the total sample. More than half of all organisations in the energy and water supply sector have 5,000 or more employees, compared with only two per cent in the engineering sector, while at least half of all organisations in construction, transport and communication, and other services, have fewer than 50 employees.

Table 1.7 Size distribution of organisations within each sector

	1–10	11–49	50–199	200–499	500–4,999	5,000+	N=
All	19.5	19.2	20.7	17.3	14.7	8.5	1,078
Energy/Water Supply	0.0	3.7	3.7	18.5	22.2	51.9	27
Metals/Minerals	9.3	6.7	28.0	26.7	21.3	8.0	75
Engineering	10.7	18.0	26.7	26.2	16.5	1.9	206
Other Manufacturing	5.9	20.6	26.5	23.5	19.1	4.4	68
Construction	23.9	32.4	21.1	11.3	8.5	2.8	71
Distribution/Hotels	19.4	19.4	20.0	18.8	13.5	8.8	170
Transport/Communication	34.5	29.1	10.0	10.0	8.2	8.2	110
Business Services	23.8	13.5	20.7	14.5	15.5	11.9	193
Other Services	27.2	22.8	17.7	8.2	13.9	10.0	158

Note: Sector SIC 0 Agriculture, Forestry and Fishing was not included – see Appendix 1, Section 1.2.

Source: IMS Survey

Institute of Manpower Studies

Appendix 2
Questionnaire

THE EMPLOYMENT OF PEOPLE WITH DISABILITIES

**A survey conducted by
the Institute of Manpower Studies**

**on behalf of
The Employment Department**

**Institute of Manpower Studies
Mantell Building
University of Sussex
Falmer, Brighton
BN1 9RF
Tel: (0273) 686751
Fax: (0273) 690430**

This survey is being conducted by the Institute of Manpower Studies (IMS) on behalf of the Employment Department, to obtain an up-to-date picture of the recruitment and employment of people with disabilities. It aims to provide Government with information on what employers are doing with regard to recruiting and employing people with disabilities, the problems faced by employers in this area, and the kinds of help and assistance they require.

We would be most grateful if you, or an appropriate colleague could complete this questionnaire, and return it to IMS in the envelope provided. Most questions simply require ticking the appropriate box, and the questionnaire should only take a short time to complete.

The survey is entirely confidential, and the data collected will be used anonymously in a statistical analysis. No names of organisations or individuals will be passed by IMS to the Employment Department or to any other party. Individual questionnaires will be destroyed after the data have been anonymously coded.

If you have any queries, please contact Nigel Meager, Sheila Honey or Clare Simkin at IMS, or Monica Haynes in our survey unit, on (0273) 686751.

The survey is about disability and employment, and we recognise that there are many definitions and perceptions of a person with a disability. For present purposes, however, a person with a disability is:
> "A person who has a disability or long-term health problem which affects the work they can do, whether they are registered as disabled or not."

Thank you in advance for your assistance

Background information about this organisation/establishment

1 Please indicate whether you are answering this questionnaire on behalf of: *(please tick one box)*

The whole organisation/business ☐   A single site or establishment ☐   Some other unit (e.g. division, region etc) ☐

2 What is the name of your organisation/business? *Please write in* _____

3 What are your main products or services? *Please write in* _____

4 In which sector is your organisation/business?   *(please tick one box)*

private sector ☐   public sector ☐   voluntary sector ☐

5 How many are currently employed in your organisation/establishment? *Please write in* ☐

Employment of people with disabilities

6 Does your organisation/establishment currently employ any people with disabilities or long-term health problems which affect the work they can do, whether they are registered as disabled or not? *Please tick one box*

Yes ☐   No ☐   Don't know ☐

If you have answered "no" or "don't know", please go to question 10

7 If "yes", how many people with disabilities do you employ? *Please write in, if known* ☐

8 And of these, how many are registered disabled? *Please write in, if known* ☐

9 Please indicate, by ticking the appropriate boxes, which types of disability you are aware of among employees in your organisation/establishment

disability affecting mobility or dexterity of arms, legs, hands, feet, back, neck or head (incl. cerebral palsy, MS, arthritis) ☐   difficulty in hearing ☐

difficulty in seeing, even when glasses, contact lenses or other aids are used ☐   skin conditions, allergies ☐

contd.

For office use only

severe heart, severe blood pressure or severe blood circulation problems		chest or breathing problems, asthma, bronchitis
		31-32

severe heart, severe blood pressure or severe blood circulation problems ☐   chest or breathing problems, asthma, bronchitis ☐   31-32

epilepsy ☐   diabetes ☐   stomach, liver, kidneys, bladder or digestion problems ☐   33-35

blood disorders, like leukemia, haemophilia or anaemia ☐   depression, bad nerves or anxiety ☐   36-37

mental illness or suffer from phobias, panics or other nervous disorders ☐   mental handicap or other severe or specific learning difficulties ☐   38-39

drug or alcohol dependency/addiction ☐   Other *(please specify)* ☐   40-41

_____   42-43

Please go to question 15

Questions 10-12 are for organisations who do <u>not</u> currently employ people with disabilities

10 If your organisation/establishment does not employ/recruit people with disabilities, is this because:

no-one with a disability has applied for employment in the organisation/establishment? ☐   *please tick those which apply*   44

some have applied, but not been recruited, on grounds other than their disability? ☐   45

some have applied, but not been recruited due to their disability, which was a barrier for a particular job? ☐   46

some have been employed in the past, but subsequently left? ☐   47

don't know ☐   other reason(s) *(please specify)* _____ ☐   48-49

50-51

11 Are there, in your view, particular problems or difficulties associated with the employment of people with disabilities?

please tick one box   Yes ☐   No ☐   Don't know ☐   52

12 If "yes", what do you feel is the source of these difficulties? *Please tick appropriate box(es)*

premises ☐   cost of special equipment ☐   cost of alterations to premises ☐   53-55

types of job/work ☐   difficult access to premises ☐   difficult journey to work ☐   56-58

attitudes of other staff/managers ☐   attitudes of customers ☐   concern about productivity of workers with disabilities ☐   59-61

concern that disabled workers might have increased sick leave ☐   concern about additional supervision/management costs ☐   62-63

Other factors *(please specify)* _____ ☐   64

65-66

13 Are there, in your view, particular problems or difficulties associated with the retention of employees who have become disabled?

please tick one box   Yes ☐   No ☐   Don't know ☐

14 If "yes", what do you feel is the source of these difficulties? _Please write in, using the categories given in question 12, if possible_

_____

All remaining questions should be answered by <u>all</u> respondents, unless otherwise indicated

Policies on recruitment/employment of people with disabilities

15 Does your organisation/establishment have a formal policy regarding the recruitment and employment of people with disabilities? _Please tick one box_

Yes, written policy ☐   Yes, unwritten policy ☐   No policy ☐   Don't know ☐

16 Does your organisation/establishment actively seek to recruit people with disabilities? _Please tick one box_

Yes ☐   No ☐   Don't know ☐

If "no" or "don't know", go to question 18

17 If "yes",

a) does this apply to:

all vacancies ☐   a specified range of vacancies ☐   specific vacancies on a case-by-case basis ☐   don't know ☐

b) how do you seek to recruit people with disabilities? _Please tick appropriate box(es)_

specific request to Jobcentre/Careers Office ☐   job advertisements welcoming disabled applicants ☐   notify Disablement Resettlement Officer/Disability Employment Adviser ☐

notifying a voluntary organisation ☐   other method(s) _(please specify)_ _____ ☐

c) does your organisation/establishment use the Employment Service disability symbol in job advertisements and recruitment literature? _Please tick one box_

Yes ☐   No ☐   Don't know ☐

Problems/difficulties encountered in employing people with disabilities

18 If a person with a disability applied for a job, what questions/reservations would be uppermost in your mind? _Please write in_

_____

_____

19 Has your organisation/establishment experienced particular problems or difficulties in the employment of people with disabilities?

please tick one box   Yes ☐   No ☐   Don't know ☐

If "no" or "don't know", go to question 21

20 If "yes", please indicate below the disabilities in question, and the nature of the problem/difficulty encountered:

problem/difficulty	**disability**
_____	_____
_____	_____
_____	_____

21 Are there specific disabilities which you feel would prevent a person being employed in your organisation/establishment? *Please tick one box*

Yes ☐ No ☐ Don't know ☐

If "no" or "don't know", go to question 23

22 If "yes", please indicate below the disabilities in question, and the reasons for the difficulty (*please use the categories of disability listed in question 9 above, if possible*)

Disability	Reason
_____	_____
_____	_____
_____	_____
_____	_____
_____	_____

Advantages of employing people with disabilities

23 Does your organisation see any benefit or advantage (to the organisation) associated with the recruitment/employment of people with disabilities?

please tick one box   Yes ☐   No ☐   Don't know ☐

If "no" or "don't know", go to question 25

24 If "yes", please give brief details (*write in*)

_____

_____

_____

_____

Actions taken and support needed in employing people with disabilities

25 Has your organisation/establishment undertaken specific actions as a result of employing people with disabilities, in order to make it feasible/safe for them to do their job, or to improve their comfort/productivity? (examples might include the provision of special or modified equipment, modification of buildings/premises, reorganisation of work/changing work content, special training, raising awareness of other staff, etc) *Please tick one box*

Yes ☐   No ☐   Don't know ☐

If "no" or "don't know", go to question 27

26 If "yes", please indicate below the disabilities in question, and the action(s) taken:

Disability	Action(s) taken
_____	_____
_____	_____
_____	_____
_____	_____
_____	_____

27 Has your organisation recently considered and rejected any of the kinds of actions outlined in question 25 above?

Please tick one box   Yes ☐   No ☐   Don't know ☐

If "no" or "don't know", go to question 29

28 If "yes", what actions were considered, and why were they rejected? *Please write in*

action considered	reason for rejection
_____	_____
_____	_____
_____	_____
_____	_____

29 Are there, or do you think there would be, any extra costs to the organisation associated with recruiting/employing people with disabilities? *Please tick one box*

Yes ☐   No ☐   Don't know ☐

30 As an example, how much extra cost would the organisation/establishment be prepared to incur as a result of recruiting a person with a disability in a post with a gross equivalent annual salary of:

a) £8,000?   initial cost (£) ☐   ongoing cost (£ per year) ☐

b) £15,000?   initial cost (£) ☐   ongoing cost (£ per year) ☐

c) £22,000?   initial cost (£) ☐   ongoing cost (£ per year) ☐

31 Would the organisation/establishment be prepared to spend more than this when the person in question was an *existing employee* acquiring a disability or long-term health problem whilst in post? *Please tick one box*

Yes ☐   No ☐   Don't know ☐

32 Has your organisation/establishment sought any form of help, support or advice with regard to the recruitment/employment of people with disabilities? *Please tick one box*

Yes ☐   No ☐   Don't know ☐

If "no" or "don't know", please go to question 35

33 If "yes", please indicate where you sought this external assistance, and the nature of the assistance provided (*tick boxes*)

Nature of assistance

Source of assistance	practical/financial	advice/information	referral to other source(s) of assistance	
DRO/DAS/PACT (see * below for definitions)	☐	☐	☐	10-12
Jobcentre	☐	☐	☐	13-15
Training and Enterprise Council	☐	☐	☐	16-18
Local Authority	☐	☐	☐	19-21
Citizens' Advice Bureau	☐	☐	☐	22-24
Other (*please specify*) _____	☐	☐	☐	25-27
				28-29

* Disablement Resettlement Officer/Disability Advisory Service/Placing, Assessment & Counselling Team

34 Please also indicate any organisations/agencies from whom you sought, but did not get, assistance relating to the recruitment/employment of people with disabilities (*tick boxes*)

DRO/DAS/PACT * ☐   Jobcentre ☐   Training and Enterprise Council ☐

Local Authority ☐   Citizens' Advice Bureau ☐   Other (*specify*) _____ ☐

35 Is there any form of help, support or advice from government or other agencies which you would find particularly helpful in the recruitment/employment of people with disabilities? *Please tick one box*

Yes ☐   No ☐   Don't know ☐

36 If "yes", please indicate briefly what kind of external assistance would be most useful (*write in*)

_____

_____

Further comments

If you have any further comments about the recruitment, employment, career development or retention of employees with disabilities in your organisation, about the kinds of help and support required, or about the actions you feel employers should undertake in order successfully to recruit/employ people with disabilities, please write them below:

Further contact

Thank you for participating in this survey. Please return the questionnaire in the reply-paid envelope to IMS at the address below.

All questionnaires will be treated in confidence

We hope to pursue the issues covered in the survey in greater depth with a small number of employers. If you or a colleague would be willing to spare a small amount of time for a confidential discussion with a member of our research team, please indicate:

Name of contact: _____   Telephone number: _____

Position in organisation: _____

If, however, you would not be prepared to be contacted again in connection with this work, please put a cross in the box: ☐

If you have any queries about the study, please contact Nigel Meager, Sheila Honey, Clare Simkin or Monica Haynes at the address below.

Institute of Manpower Studies
Mantell Building
University of Sussex
Falmer, Brighton
BN1 9RF
Tel: (0273) 686751
Fax: (0273) 690430

Appendix 3
Literature Review

1. Introduction

The research project, of which this literature review forms part, examines through a postal survey of employers and subsequent in–depth interviews, the attitudes and behaviour of employers towards people with disabilities. In particular, the main rationale for the research is to obtain a much clearer idea of what employers are prepared to do with regard to recruiting and employing people with disabilities, with emphasis on *why* 'leading edge' employers are prepared to act (which in turn will provide a source of advice and guidance for other employers), and the areas in which employers are *not* prepared to act. The Government also needs to discover what kinds of help and assistance employers need if they are to do more in this area.

Normal practice in such projects for the IMS Commentary programme is to conduct an initial review of existing relevant literature and data, to inform the design of the research instruments, and to sit the findings of the study in the context of what is already known. In the present case, however, there was some question as to whether the answers to the questions being covered in the study could be obtained from previous research. The literature/data review, therefore, had the additional function of checking whether this was the case, and whether the subsequent planned stage of primary empirical research could be justified. For this reason, it was agreed that this short interim report, summarising the findings of the literature review would be produced at an early stage of the research.

As will be seen from this summary, there is a considerable range of existing research on disability and employment, but there is little up–to–date evidence on employers' practice, and attitudes, and what there is does not go beyond the case–study level at best, and anecdote at worst. Our judgement on the basis of the literature/data review, therefore, is that the case for the primary empirical research being undertaken remains strong.

The research undertaken for the literature/data review was structured around the following issues:

- the distribution of different types of disability (in the population at large and in employment);

- evidence from each main type of disability of what employers *are recommended* to do on behalf of the disabled (*eg* by the various charities and bodies acting on behalf of people with disabilities);

- evidence of what employers actually do;

- why do they do it?

- any differentiation between what employers do for new recruits and what they do for existing employees?

- costs incurred/ problems encountered;

- employers who do not employ/do anything for disabled – why?

- role of government support/codes of practice/disability symbols *etc.*

2. Distribution of Different Types of Disability

An initial task was to attempt to establish the prevalence of disability in the population as a whole and the workforce itself, and then to examine the prevalence of different types of disability. It was felt that such information would be useful to set against employers' perceptions of the prevalence of disability, and to inform the design of research instruments (at the case–study stage, in particular, where it was intended to examine employers' attitudes through the use of examples, this would assist the choice of such examples).

There is a wealth of data documenting the numbers of people with disabilities in general, and with specific disabilities (many of the data and information sources are usefully summarised in the papers in *Dalley, 1991*). Many of these data are at best inconsistent, and at worst contradictory. Enormous problems arise due to:

● the difficulty of defining disability;

● its relative nature (what counts as a disability can be heavily influenced by how disabling is the environment in which the person in question finds him/herself);

● the question of who is doing the defining (the person presumed to be disabled may come up with very different definitions from an external agency);

● the difficulty of distinguishing disability from other states (such as 'long term ill–health'); and

● the wide range of specific definitions used to describe particular people's conditions (varying from medical descriptions of the condition in question, to descriptions of the implications of its symptoms for the person's functioning in society).

In this section we summarise the maze of statistics on disability incidence in the UK, concentrating on the main findings from the most important sources.

Two general points about how the prevalence of disability may vary are also worth making.

● Firstly, however disability is defined, *the prevalence of many types of disability increases with age*, for obvious reasons. This means that overall estimates of the incidence of disability in the population will be very sensitive to how that population is defined. If we include the whole population, for example, we will get much larger estimates of the proportion of people with disabilities than if we confine ourselves to people of working age. Similarly, the percentage of people with disabilities in the client group of particular training programmes will depend very much on the age–eligibility rules of that programme;

● secondly, it might be expected that for many types of disability, there will be no tendency for their incidence to vary systematically between different parts of the country. Nevertheless, insofar as some types of disability (*eg* learning difficulties) are correlated with social and economic deprivation, there is reason to expect that areas which score highly on indices of multiple deprivation in their populations will also contain higher than average proportions of people with these kinds of disability.

2.1 Incidence of disability in the population as a whole

In order to obtain data on the incidence of disability in the population, the Office of Population Censuses and Surveys (OPCS) conducted a series of interview surveys in 1985 and 1986, covering 14,000 adults with disabilities and the parents of 1,300 disabled children (the surveys are reported in *Martin, Meltzer and Elliott, 1988; Martin and White, 1988; Bone and Meltzer, 1989; Martin, White and Meltzer 1989; Smyth and Robus, 1989; Meltzer, Smyth and Robus, 1989*).

The OPCS work (which has been criticised for its adherence to the 'medical model' of disability) distinguishes between 'Impairment', 'Disability' and 'Handicap' according to the International Classification of Impairments, Disabilities and Handicaps (ICIDH)[11], and OPCS concentrate on 'Disability' under this definition, although information on the other two categories was also collected.

On the basis of these surveys, and taking account also of information from the General Household Survey, grossed up to the population as

---

[11] The relevant definitions are as follows:
Impairment – any loss or abnormality of psychological, physiological or anatomical structure or function (*ie* this is dealing with parts or systems of the body that do not work);
Disability – any restriction or lack (resulting from an impairment) of ability to perform an activity in the manner or within the range considered normal for a human being (*ie* this refers to things people cannot do);
Handicap – a disadvantage for a given individual, resulting from an impairment or disability, that limits or prevents the fulfilment of a role (depending on age, sex or cultural factors) for that individual (*ie* this is in relation to a particular environment and relationships with other people).

In many cases there is a one–to–one correspondence between impairment and disability if the impairment is sufficiently serious. *Eg* an impairment with vision will give rise to a disability with seeing and a handicap regarding orientation. However, to complicate matters, two different impairments can lead to the same disability, or one impairment can give rise to several disabilities. Thus skeletal and cardio–respiratory impairments can both lead to disability in walking. There is also a lack of correspondence between disability and handicap, as handicaps are affected by factors such as differences in the environment, the availability of support from others, and the roles an individual is expected to fill.

a whole, OPCS estimated that there were 6,560,000 people with disabilities in Great Britain in 1985. This is equivalent to just over 12 per cent of the population, or one in eight.

2.1.1 Incidence of disability among people of working age

Of more interest for present purposes is the incidence of disability in the population of working age (*ie* between 16 and 60/65). Here we have at least three major sources of data: the OPCS survey mentioned above; a survey of 'Employment and Handicap' conducted for the Employment Service by Social and Community Planning Research (SCPR) in 1989 *(Prescott–Clarke, 1990)*; and the regular Labour Force Survey (LFS), conducted annually until 1992 (since when it has been quarterly), which contains a set of questions asking people about health problems or disabilities which limit the kind of work they can do.

Table 1 below looks first at the most recent data available (from the Labour Force Survey in March–May 1992), on disability amongst people of working age.

Table 1. Disability and economic activity (Spring 1992)

(millions)	Population of working age	In employment	Unemployed	Economically inactive
Total	35.01	24.86	2.70	7.45
With a limiting health problem or disability	4.66	1.80	0.46	2.39
% disabled	13.30	7.30	16.90	32.10

Source: IMS calculations from Labour Force Survey

Key features of note are:

● the LFS suggests that there are just over four and a half million people of working age with a health problem or disability which limits the kind of work they can do (this is based on the self–assessment of the individuals themselves).

● this represents 13 per cent of the working age population, but the incidence of disability is much lower than this amongst those in employment (seven per cent), and much higher amongst the unemployed (17 per cent) and the economically inactive (32 per cent). Put another way, this confirms earlier findings that the disabled are much more likely than other people to be unemployed or out of the labour market altogether.

How do these LFS data compare with the earlier data from other sources? Table 2 shows comparable data from the OPCS (1985) survey, the SCPR (1989), and also includes earlier data from the 1989 LFS in order to provide comparison between at least two sources from the same year.

Table 2. Disability and economic activity: different sources compared

Disabled (millions)	OPCS (1985)	SCPR (1989)	LFS (1989)	LFS (1992)
Total disabled of working age	2.11	2.71	n.a.	4.66
Economically inactive	1.25	1.44	n.a.	2.39
of which: permanently unable to work	*0.72*	*n.a.*	*n.a.*	*n.a.*
Unemployed	0.21	0.28	0.40	0.46
In employment	0.65	0.99	1.85	1.80
Unemployment rate (%)				
disabled	24.4	22.0	17.7	20.2
total population	n.a.	n.a.	7.2	9.8
'non–employment' rate (%)				
disabled	69.2	63.5	n.a.	61.2
total population	n.a.	n.a.	n.a.	29.0

Source: IMS compilation

The Table confirms the enormous differences between the different sources, and comparing the LFS and the SCPR data for the same year (1989) shows that these differences do not simply reflect the different time period during which the data were collected. Rather they reflect the differences in definition used in the different surveys. It is clear that the LFS definition is much broader than that used by the other sources[12], including as it does limiting health problems which would not always have been categorised as a disability in the other sources. This yields an estimate of the disabled population of working age which is almost twice as large as that given in the OPCS and SCPR surveys. The OPCS survey, with the most restrictive definition, produces the smallest estimates of disability.

All the different sources, however, confirm the labour market disadvantage of the disabled, and in all cases the disabled have much higher rates of unemployment and of economic inactivity than does the working age population as a whole. Interestingly, the more restrictive the definition of disability (*ie* the more we exclude those with 'limiting health problems'), the greater that relative disadvantage seems to be. Thus the unemployment rate for the disabled is highest in the OPCS survey (which adopted the tightest definition of disability), and lowest in the LFS (even in the latter case, however, it

---

[12]   It is of interest to note, that the first results of the 1991 Population Census, which included for the first time a question on 'limiting long–term illness', produces an figure of 13.1 per cent for the population as a whole, which is close to the LFS estimates discussed here (see *OPCS 1992*).

is more than twice as high as the unemployment rate in the labour force as a whole). This suggests that the 'hard core' of people with disabilities are the most disadvantaged in labour market terms. A similar pattern was confirmed within the OPCS data set, since OPCS classified individuals on a scale according to the severity of the disability, and the results showed clearly that the more severe the disability, the greater the likelihood of being unemployed.

Table 2 also shows the 'non–employment' rates for disabled people – *ie* it takes those not in work as a proportion of the total working age population (i.e. including the economically inactive). Again, all the sources show that between 60 and 70 per cent of the disabled population of working age are not in work at any one time, a figure which is more than twice as high as that for the working age population as a whole. It might be thought that economically inactive people with disabilities are out of the workforce because they are permanently unable to work. The OPCS survey, however, showed that this applied to only just over a half of the economically inactive people with disabilities, suggesting a significant reservoir of disabled people who would be able to work, but do not seek work, because they are 'discouraged' or do not believe they would get a job.

It is clear that the LFS, despite its relatively broad definition of disability, is a mine of under-utilised information on the experiences of people with disabilities in the labour market, their education and qualifications, the training they undertake, their regional distribution, and the extent to which they are affected by recession. We have been unable, in the short time available for preparation of the present paper, to undertake a full analysis of the LFS.

We were, able, however, to begin to examine the question of the extent to which the disabled are disproportionately affected by recession. Figure 1 shows how the unemployment[13] rate for people with limiting health problems or disability has moved since 1988, in comparison with the overall unemployment rate. It suggests that although people with disabilities have much higher unemployment rates than average, their unemployment rates are *less volatile than average over the economic cycle*. That is to say, when the economy was booming, as in 1988–90, people with disabilities benefited to a lesser than average extent from the fall in unemployment. The converse of this, however, is that in recession (post–1990) the unemployment rate of people with disabilities appears to have increased less fast than the average.

2.1.2 Regional variations

There is some evidence of inter–regional variation in the incidence of limiting health problems and disability, although one would expect that this variation would be mainly due to variations in health problems and disabilities which are correlated with socio–economic conditions. The data are not detailed enough to check this supposition, however.

---

[13]   The LFS uses the international standard (ILO/OECD) definition of unemployment, rather than the UK registered unemployment definition.

Figure 1. Unemployed rates 1988-92

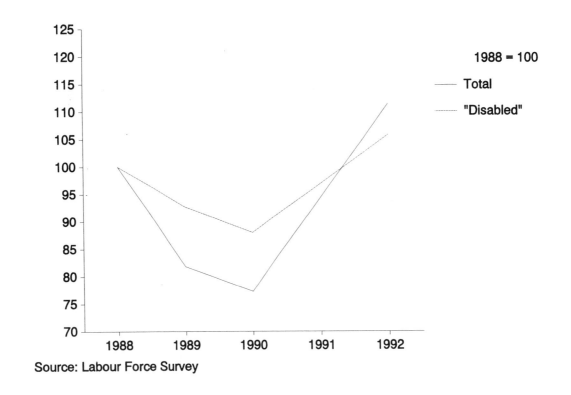

Source: Labour Force Survey

The 1991 Census results (*OPCS 1992*), show that the percentage of persons with a limiting long–term illness is 13.1 per cent for Britain as a whole, but that this varies from a high of 17.1 per cent in Wales to a low of 10.0 per cent in the Outer Metropolitan area of the South East. Generally the incidence appears to increase as one moves West and North from London and the South East. A similar regional analysis can be undertaken from the LFS, although time did not permit this for the present paper. We understand, however, that a regional analysis of the incidence of limiting health problems and disability has been undertaken internally by the Employment Department (due to be published shortly), which shows broadly the same pattern as that revealed by the Census above.

An analysis from the LFS (over 1988–90) of relative unemployment rates of people with disabilities reported in *Johnson, 1992*, showed some regional variations in those unemployment rates, but these variations were generally in line with the overall regional patterns of unemployment. That is, regions with a higher than average overall unemployment rate tended also to have a higher than average unemployment rate among people with disabilities, an *vice versa*. Interestingly, the inter–regional variation in unemployment rates among people with disabilities appeared to be considerably less than that among the population as a whole. In other words the labour market disadvantage of those with disabilities was more uniform across regions than might have been expected given the inter–regional variation in general labour market conditions.

2.2 Variation by skill level and occupation

All data sources confirm that people with disabilities tend to have lower levels of education, qualification and skills than the average, and those of them in employment tend to be concentrated in low–paid, low–skilled and low–status jobs. This provides a strong *prima facie* case for training interventions having a crucial role in improving the labour market position of people with disabilities.

The most comprehensive data source on these issues (the LFS) has yet to be fully utilised, but data from the SCPR survey reported in the Employment Department consultative document on employment and training for people with disabilities (*Employment Department, 1990*) show a relative lack of formal qualifications among people with disabilities in work — 42 per cent have no qualifications compared with 32.2 per cent of non–disabled people, and among people with disabilities who are out of work, but wanting work, the figure is even higher (59 per cent — see *Prescott-Clarke, 1990*).

Table 3 looks at the kind of jobs disabled people get, and again the different sources paint a consistent picture. Compared with the general working population (as indicated by data from the General Household Survey — GHS), people with disabilities are less likely to be employed in higher level occupations. Given the general trend towards an increasing proportion of jobs being in white collar occupations, and highly skilled occupations, this suggests that without significant on–going training input, people with disabilities are at a disproportionate risk of being disadvantaged by likely future changes in the structure of employment.

Table 3. Disability by occupation

Occupational group	People with disabilities		General population	
	OPCS 1985	SCPR 1989	GHS 1985	GHS 1987
	%	%	%	%
Professional or managerial	13	12	20	21
Other white collar	30	30	33	33
Skilled manual	26	26	25	25
Semi–skilled manual and personal service	22	25	18	16
Unskilled manual	9	6	5	5
Total	100	100	100	100

Source: IMS Survey

2.3 Prevalence of different types of disability

The classification of different types of disability is a complex and controversial area, and many would argue that the language of disability, and the 'medical model' often used to classify disabilities, or the impairments which lead to disabilities, have been important contributors to reinforcing negative stereotypes of people with disabilities, and perpetuating their disadvantages in society and the labour market (for a useful discussion of these issues see Chapter 1 in *Dalley, 1990*).

Whilst we accept many of these arguments, we would nevertheless argue that there is some value in the attempt at classifying and quantifying different types of disability. In order to understand what type of provision needs to be made for people with disabilities, it is necessary to understand the types of disabilities people have, and how these disabilities affect the kinds of work they can do.

2.3.1 Data from voluntary and charitable bodies on specific disabilities

The common public perception of different types of disabilities appears to be heavily influenced by the various voluntary organisations and charities providing support and information on these disabilities — *eg* cerebral palsy, cystic fibrosis, diabetes, Downs syndrome, epilepsy, haemophilia, leukaemia, multiple sclerosis, Parkinson's disease, spina bifida *etc.* (a useful glossary of key facts about many of these disabilities and conditions is provided in *Training Agency, 1989*). The various voluntary organisations (with a few notable exceptions, such as the Royal National Institute for the Blind) do not themselves, for the most part, conduct thorough surveys of the numbers of people affected by the disabilities and conditions they cover. We have nevertheless attempted, by contacting as many as possible of the various disability organisations, and consulting other sources to put together approximate estimates of the numbers of people affected by the main disability types — because they are compiled from so many different sources, the figures are not directly comparable one with the other (most data refer to the whole population rather than people of working age, and are thus inflated for present purposes, since they include large numbers of older people with higher incidences of disability). They do nevertheless provide some indication of which disabilities (and complaints which may lead to disability) are the most widespread, and which the least widespread.

Table 4. Estimates of prevalence of specific disabilities

Disability	Numbers affected	Source of information
Arthritis	15,000 children 5% of 16–44 year olds 20% of 45–64 year olds 40 per cent of 65+ Estimated 20m sufferers p.a. 8m p.a. consult doctor (200 thousand with rheumatic fever)	Arthritis care
Deafness	20% have hearing difficulties 5% use hearing aids 24,000 registered disabled 1.4m adults of working age have clinically significant hearing loss	RNID
Diabetes	750,000 diagnosed 250,000 estimate undiagnosed	British Diabetic Association
Blindness	300,000 blind 457,000 partially sighted But *NB*, RNIB estimate 91,000 blind/partially sighted people *of working age*	RNIB
Mental Illness	25% of the population at some time 10% will be treated as an in–patient at some time	MIND, Employment Service
Mental Handicap (severe learning difficulties)	Between 1 and 1.5 million	MENCAP
Moderate learning difficulties	Between 0.5% and 1.5% of a given age group	Rathbone Society
Spina Bifida	10% of population, but most not affected. 1.7 per 10,000 births	Association for Spina Bifida and Hydrocephalus
Hydrocephalus	1.3 per 10,000 births ABSAH knows of 15,000 families with spina bifida and/or hydrocephalus	
Epilepsy	1 in 200	British Epilepsy Association
Parkinson's Disease	120,000 1 in 1,000 under 65 1 in 100 over 65 1 in 50 over 8 1 in 7 of those diagnosed are under 40	Parkinson's Disease Society
Down's Syndrome	1 in 800 1 in 700 of live births in UK	Down's Syndrome Association
Head Injury	70,000	National Head Injuries Association
Multiple Sclerosis	80,000 in UK	Multiple Sclerosis Society
Cystic Fibrosis	1 in 20 carry the gene 6,000 affected in 1992	Cystic Fibrosis Research Trust
Haemophilia	around 1 in 5,000 males 8,858 recorded cases	Haemophilia Society
Huntington's Chorea	6,000	Huntington's Disease Association
Amputations	New amputations in 1989: 166 upper limb, 4,041 lower limb (*total data not yet uncovered*	National Assoc. for Limbless Disabled

Disability	Numbers affected	Source of information
Sickle Cell Anaemia	1 in 200 of susceptible population 6,000 sufferers in Britain	Sickle Cell Society
Polio	No data available	British Polio Fellowship
Muscular Dystrophy	1 per 3,000 of population approximately 18,300	Muscular Dystrophy Group of Great Britain
Cerebral Palsy	1,500 each year one in every 400	Spastics Society *continued/*
Spinal Injury	No data available	Spinal Injuries Association
Stroke	150,000 disabled by stroke at any one time 120,000 suffer a stroke each year 10,000 are under age of 65	British Heart Foundation

Source: compiled by IMS from sources listed

2.3.2 Data from official national surveys

Unfortunately, such commonly used categories do not correspond with the detailed classification systems used in the various official surveys (OPCS, SCPR, GHS, LFS *etc.*), typically based on a medical model of the underlying impairment leading to disability, rather than the disability itself.

There are several approaches which have been adopted in recent national surveys. The SCPR 'Employment and Handicap' survey of 1989 (*Prescott–Clarke, 1990*), adopted a classification based on the notion of *complaints leading to an occupational handicap*. Again this was based on the International Classification of Diseases, and was designed to be consistent with the coding systems used by Employment Service staff when recording details of clients with disabilities.

Table 5 summarises the results from the SCPR study. Column (a) shows the complaints identified by the respondent as the *main cause* of their occupational handicap, whilst column (b) shows *all the complaints* which they regarded as contributing to that handicap. It is important to note that many people with disabilities have more than one disability, and in the SCPR survey around a third of respondents named more than one condition as giving rise to an occupational handicap.

Nearly half of the economically active sample reported a problem with their musculo–skeletal system, and for 41 per cent this was the main complaint (for 16 per cent, this arose from arthritis or rheumatism). The second largest group of complaints (affecting 16 per cent of the sample) were to do with the respiratory system, whilst circulatory complaints were cited by 13 per cent.

Table 5. Incidence of complaints leading to occupational handicap

Complaints (ICD groups)	Percentage of economically active respondents with disabilities	
	a) 'main complaint' leading to occupational handicap	b) 'all complaints' leading to occupational handicap
musculo–skeletal system	41	48
respiratory system	11	16
heart and circulation system	8	13
mental disorders	7	11
nervous system	7	8
eye complaints/defects	5	7
ear complaints/defects	4	7
digestive system	4	6
skin disease or disorders	4	6
endocrine and metabolic	3	4
neoplasms	2	2
genito–urinary	1	2
blood & bloodforming agents	*	1
infections and parasitic	*	*
congenital abnormalities	*	*
other, ill–defined and vague	3	4
Total	100	100

Note: column b) does not total 100% as respondents could cite more than one complaint
   * indicates less than 1%

Source: IMS Survey

Table 5a Main types of complaints leading to a disability among the economically active (% citing each type of complaint)

limbs, back or head	52		hearing	9
respiration	18		sight	7
circulation	13	mental handicap	3	
digestion	10	mental illness	3	
depression/anxiety	10			

Source: Employment and Handicap 1990

The SCPR results have been further reclassified by the Employment Department into a simpler, more intuitive grouping of the main complaints leading to occupational handicap (*Employment Department, 1990*), and this classification is presented in Table 5a.

Perhaps a more useful approach to present these figures is not in terms of the underlying complaint, but in terms of the type of disability resulting from the complaints. The SCPR data have also been reclassified in such a fashion and the results are given in Table 6 (again the figures exceed 100 per cent since many respondents had more than one disability).

Table 6. Type of disability reported by economically active people with disabilities

Disability	% of economically active citing this disability
locomotion	40
hearing	20
intellectual functioning	19
behaviour	18
dexterity	16
seeing	14
communication	9
eating, drinking, digestion	9
continence	8
disfigurement	7
reaching and stretching	6
consciousness	4

Source: Prescott-Clarke, 1990

There is not an obvious one–to–one correspondence between the data in Tables 5 and 6; thus Table 6 shows larger proportions of people with disabilities in seeing and hearing, than are given as having eye and ear complaints in Table 5. A key reason for this is that similar disabilities may result from very different underlying complaints (diabetes, for example, might give rise to a visual disability).

Problems to do with walking, climbing stairs and maintaining balance account for 40 per cent of economically active people with disabilities. The next most common problems are those to do with hearing (accounting for 20 per cent), and intellectual functioning (accounting for 19 per cent). Disabilities relating to behaviour, dexterity and vision are also important.

Finally, we turn again to the Labour Force survey, which uses yet another categorisation of 'limiting health problems and disabilities' (although one which is broadly related to that given in Table 5a above). The particular advantage of this source is that it enables us not only to look at the incidence of disability among people of working age, but also at the labour market position of people with different types of limiting health problem or disability. Table 7 presents the relevant data from the spring 1992 LFS. The data are broadly consistent with those of the other sources: with musculo–skeletal and similar problems by far the most prevalent, followed by respiratory and circulatory problems. These three categories between them account for the main problem of some two thirds of those people with limiting health problems or disabilities.

Table 7 also reveals considerable variation in the unemployment rates experienced by people with the various different problems; varying from 12.3 per cent among those with circulatory difficulties to 38.9 per cent among those reporting 'depression or bad nerves'. The unemployment rate is not the only measure of labour market disadvantage, however, and as can be seen by examining the 'non–employment' rate data in the Table some categories with relatively low unemployment rates have high rates of economic inactivity (implying that most of those who cannot get jobs, tend to withdraw from the labour market — this is true of those with circulatory problems, for example). On the other hand some categories with relatively high unemployment rates have relatively low economic inactivity rates (implying that most of these people who cannot get jobs remain in the labour market, searching for work — perhaps because they are not eligible for invalidity benefit *etc.* — this is true, for example, of those with skin conditions and allergies).

Table 7. Incidence of limiting health problems & disabilities & economic activity

Source of health problem/disability (main problem only)	Number affected	% of working age population	% of those with disabilities	unemployment rate (%)	'non–employment' rate (%)
arms, legs, hands, feet, back, neck	1,975,976	5.6	42.4	19.5	60.6
chest, breathing problems	617,599	1.8	13.3	22.7	56.4
heart, blood pressure, circulation	508,283	1.5	10.9	12.3	65.7
depression, bad nerves	235,764	0.7	5.1	38.9	85.3
stomach, liver, kidney, digestion	202,435	0.6	4.3	24.0	65.9
diabetes	158,790	0.5	3.4	15.8	44.9
difficulty in seeing	154,334	0.4	3.3	21.7	53.8
difficulty in hearing	130,504	0.4	2.8	17.1	42.7
skin conditions, allergies	120,902	0.3	2.6	24.1	47.7
epilepsy	110,033	0.3	2.4	19.9	61.2
other problems, disabilities	442,033	1.3	9.5	24.0	68.5
Total with health problems/disabilities	4,656,653	13.3	100.0	20.2	61.2

Source: IMS calculations from Labour Force Survey

2.4 Impact of disability on work performance

The final area of importance with regard to employment is the limitations the disability places on work performance. The SCPR survey found that the majority (78 per cent) of the economically active were able to work a five day week and a seven or eight hour day. Of the 20 per cent not able to work a full day, half could work for four or more hours a day and those not able to work a full week (12%), half could work three or four days a week. With regard to time off due to sickness or treatment, the majority of economically active (46%) claimed to take less than five days a year although one in ten took thirty or more days. When asked about periods of sickness over a month in the last five years, 52 per cent had had no such spell and 32 per cent had only done so once or twice. About a quarter of those economically active would have to take regular breaks from work at least once a day but the breaks were mostly short. Twenty eight per cent of those in work found that there were some tasks normally part of their job that they could not perform. Most of these thus needed help to do their job but over half needed help only occasionally (*Prescott–Clarke, 1990*).

Finally, the SCPR study found that 64 per cent of people with disabilities interviewed felt that they got about the same amount of work done as the general population. Sixteen per cent said they did more. The disadvantages of employing a person with a disability are probably nowhere near as great as employers perceive.

3. What is Good Practice in Employing People with Disabilities?

There has been a great deal written as to what employers should do in order to improve the opportunities for people with disabilities. The majority of the voluntary organisations have guides written to aid employers overcome the problems presented by each particular disability. Less specifically, most trades unions provide their own guidelines to avoid discrimination both in recruitment and in the work–place (*NALGO, SOGAT, BIFU, TUC*). In addition there is a very detailed handbook produced by the Institute of Personnel Management (*Birkett & Worman, 1988*). Central to all these however, is the 'Code of Good Practice on the Employment of Disabled People' produced by the Employment Service (*Employment Service, revised 1990*). This is addressed to those responsible for day to day recruitment and employment matters and brings together information on good practices which have already helped some employers.

3.1 The code of good practice

The code sets out some very general guidelines concerning methods of ensuring that employers attract applications from people with disabilities and that the procedures are fair to these workers. The code also raises certain issues regarding induction, health and safety and integration which affect employees with disabilities. It also covers the slightly different concerns which arise when an employee becomes disabled. We summarise below some of the main points from the code.

3.1.1 Recruiting people with disabilities

Job descriptions: Some requirements for a job may inadvertently exclude certain people with disabilities so they should be carefully considered as to whether they are essential and if they are flexible it should be clearly stated so.

Recruitment: Sources of recruitment should be used which are well placed to put the employer in touch with people with disabilities such as the Job Centre DRO, special schools and organisations.

Advertising: Advertisements should contain a statement welcoming disabled applicants to ensure the employer is recognised as offering fair opportunities and to encourage suitable workers with disabilities to apply. The same applies to other methods of recruitment such as private agencies.

Application and selection procedures: It is not unreasonable for an employer to ask about any disability which is relevant to the job in question. This will allow assessment of any special help which may be needed. It should however be carefully considered as to whether the information asked for is necessary and it should be made clear that admitting to a disability does not preclude full consideration for the job.

Application forms: Wording of application forms should always encourage or be positive towards applicants with disabilities.

Interviewing candidates: All suitably qualified candidates with disabilities should be interviewed since this is the only effective means of assessing their employment potential. This is especially important if an organisation is below its quota.

This will create the need for practical arrangements to be made such as holding interviews in an accessible part of the building, allowing the use of interpreters *etc*. When arranging an interview the opportunity should be taken to gain prior knowledge of any disability and possible handicap which may have to be discussed.

The interview: It should be emphasised that the disability does not affect the consideration the candidate receives in order to put them at ease. Assumptions should not be made as to what an individual can or cannot do. The interview should concentrate on ability and provide an opportunity for demonstration.

Health screening: People with disabilities should be considered in the same way as other people regarding policy on health screening. They should not be excluded from a job because it is thought that screening will lead to their rejection. Medical examinations may well dispel doubts regarding fitness, safety or severity of a handicap.

3.1.2 People with disabilities at work

Induction: It should be considered as to whether there are any special induction requirements for a person with a disability and these should be discussed fully with the person concerned and the appropriate manager. A blind person may require extra help to get to know the layout of the premises for example.

Health and safety: Employers should ascertain whether additional provision needs to be made over and above normal procedures. Two people should for example, be assigned to a person with mobility difficulties.

Integration: Acceptance by colleagues should be made as easy as possible. Supervisors should be informed of the disability and any special assistance necessary. It should be discussed with employees whether colleagues should be given this information. They should however, be given a copy of the code.

Training and promotion opportunities: People with disabilities should receive the same opportunities for training as others even if it means making special arrangements. Promotion should be awarded on ability as with any other employee. The arguments which claim disability might handicap performance at a higher grade should be examined carefully. If performance is not as good as hoped different work methods, re–structuring the job or use of special aids should be considered.

Redundancy: Every effort should be made to re–deploy staff elsewhere if possible, and offer as much help as possible in finding another job, since people with disabilities tend to remain unemployed for longer periods.

3.1.3 Assisting employees who become disabled

Keeping staff who have become disabled is clearly an advantage to an employer since it allows them to retain a valuable asset. The actions necessary to help someone return to work or retain their job will vary enormously depending on the individual case. It is essential therefore that employer keeps in regular touch with the employee to monitor their progress. It is also important to discuss at an early stage any implications for salary, pension and terms of employment. Any changes to these should be based as far as possible on agreement between the employer and the employee.

Continuing in the same job: It is often possible for an individual to remain in the same job with little or no special provision being made. Any concerns as to their ability can be covered by financial support for a trial period through the Job Introduction Scheme. In other cases special steps may be necessary. These may be provision of special aids or adaptations to the premises, or restructuring the job so that certain tasks which the individual can no longer do can be carried out by someone else.

A return to alternative work: If an employee can not return to their previous job, they should be considered for alternative work and re–training offered where necessary. Restructuring the alternative job should also be considered.

Part–time work: A return to full time work may not be possible perhaps for example due to the need to take time off for treatment. Effort should be made to offer the employee a part–time post or create one through job splitting or job sharing. Grants are available to assist in doing this.

Sheltered placement schemes: If the individual is no longer able to maintain an acceptable level of output, use of the Special Placement Scheme allows the employee to be employed by a host organisation such as a local authority or voluntary organisation and they are made available to the employer for a payment based on the level of output.

A delayed return to work: An individual may not be able to return to work immediately, or a suitable position may not be available but they should be kept on the books and regular contact made. What is essential is that the situation is kept flexible and that time is allowed for the individual to adjust to any new circumstances. A trial period to assess fully whether the employee can cope may be necessary, provision for working at home especially in the initial stages of returning to work and a gradual return to full–time hours may be advisable.

Financial and other considerations: As far as possible pay, terms of employment and pension rights should be safeguarded if a new or re–structured job is undertaken.

Termination of employment: Termination of employment may be the only realistic option but should as far as possible be in agreement with the employee. Consultations should be made with the DRO and checks made that all medical evidence has been taken into account and that there is no breach of legislation.

3.2 Other sources of good practice information

3.2.1 Employment Service guides for specific disabilities

The Code of Good Practice is a very general guide out of necessity because of the great variety of situations it is attempting to cover. To cover more specific problems the Employment Service produce a series of leaflets called 'Employing People with Disabilities' which look at particular disabilities and their effects on employment. These define the disability involved, its effects on the individual and what courses of action an employer can take to improve opportunities for someone with this particular disability. They also offer advice on issues such as insurance and pensions as well as listing special schemes available and other organisations which can offer help. The areas covered are:

Blind and Visually Impaired
Multiple Sclerosis
Deaf and Hearing Impaired
Epilepsy
Mental Illness
Mental Handicap
Haemophilia

Again we summarise some of the key recommendations below:

Blind and visually impaired

● Provide a nominated helper for the worker especially to help in an emergency.

● Make provision for a guide dog if necessary.

● Consider using special aids such as braille typewriter or switchboard with synthetic speech.

● Extra induction time and special help to gain knowledge of the building layout.

Multiple Sclerosis

- Work patterns or flow should be changed to avoid stress or physical effort.

- More breaks should be allowed and a chance to sit down if standing jobs cannot be made sedentary.

- Work should be arranged to be on the same level to avoid climbing stairs.

- One or two colleagues should be designated to help with mobility problems in an emergency.

Epilepsy

- Stress should be avoided since this can bring on attacks as should making a fuss over the condition, since this will also encourage attacks.

- Other employees should be made aware of what to do if an attack takes place, such as loosening clothing around the neck, no objects hard or soft to be inserted into the mouth *etc*. If other employees do not understand what is happening it can be disconcerting.

- Time for a rest after a major fit should be given.

Mental illness

- It should always be assumed that most people can be treated just as with physical illness. If the illness becomes severe medical advice should be sought.

- Unpredictable or unacceptable behaviour should be dealt with firmly but sympathetically bearing in mind people who are recovering from illnesses may be over–sensitive to criticism.

- Employers should be alert for any tail–off in performance, change in manner, or the development of strange behaviour. Should this occur, seek medical advice.

Mental handicap

- Sympathetic supervisors should be chosen who are patient and realise that people with learning difficulties like to know and be told that they are doing a good job.

- The employee will not only need guiding and training on the job to be done but also on patterns of behaviour and relationships with others.

- Instructions should be given carefully and patiently and be prepared to repeat. Visual instructions are more easily understood. Jobs should be broken down more than usual and not taught all at once.

- Rules need to be carefully explained at the beginning. Regular reminders of their importance and practice of safety procedures should be used to aid learning.

- Some will not be able to read but can recognise signs such as 'toilet'. Simple visual symbols might however be used instead.

- All efforts should be made to make sure they are not teased or bullied.

Deaf and hearing impaired

- Efforts should be made to speak slowly without exaggerating or shouting. Ensure that you are clearly visible.

- Messages or instructions should be written in short sentences using simple words. If an individual has been deaf from birth they will probably have limited vocabulary. Idioms and colloquialisms should be avoided.

- Attempt not to become impatient, it will make the speaker less intelligible.

- Check the employee has their hearing aid turned on. Many switch them off in noisy surroundings.

- Excessive background noise should be limited especially in meetings.

- The use of oval or circular seating will improve lip readers' views.

- Employers should learn some signs and finger spelling.

- Use of special aids should be considered *eg* amplified handsets for telephones, flashing lights or louder bells, telephone text terminals with a keyboard and screen to display textual information.

3.2.2 Guides from voluntary organisations

Many of the voluntary organisations also provide their own very specific guidelines for the particular illness in which they specialise and the disabilities and handicaps which result.

For example, the *Employer's Guide to Cystic Fibrosis (Cystic Fibrosis Trust, 1989)* states that a sufferer can normally undertake most jobs. All that is required is that they avoid dusty or similarly contaminated environments and are allowed a small number of days special leave each year so that the person may attend a specialist centre for the regular and routine examinations.

With *diabetes*, again there are few restrictions to working other than providing breaks so that the individual can receive doses of insulin when necessary and take snacks to maintain appropriate blood glucose levels. In order to avoid the very small risks of faintness and blackout due to low blood glucose levels, people should avoid situations where they would be in danger should this occur, for example very isolated situations, high ladders or platforms and closeness to moving machinery (*British Diabetic Association, 1990*).

For *haemophilia* sufferers, there are similarly few jobs which they are not able to perform. Generally occupations which are physically demanding with potential risk of injury to the joints should be avoided. Should injury occur, time should be made available for the individual to administer concentrates, thus ensuring that very little time is lost through health problems. A record should be kept of the address, name of contact and telephone number of the appropriate Haemophilia Centre in case of emergency (*Haemophilia Society, 1991*).

With virtually every guide produced, the underlying message to employers is that the most important course of action is for them to gain a full understanding of the disorder and resulting disability, to be sympathetic to the individual's problem and to make sure these problems are discussed fully with the individual. These simple measures can make a great deal of difference.

4. What do Employers Actually do when Recruiting or Employing People with Disabilities?

Government legislation to encourage employers to provide opportunities for people with disabilities was introduced under the 1944 Act as a Quota Scheme. This requires employers with 20 or more employees to employ three per cent of staff from people registered disabled unless they obtain a permit not to do so for what is assessed as a valid reason.

Over the years it has become increasingly apparent that this system is not working with the numbers of employers satisfying the quota consistently falling. In 1985, 28.1 per cent of employers had filled the quota. This was down to 22.8 per cent by 1989 *(Hansard, 21.3.90 col. 607)*.

4.1 Previous employer surveys

Studies concentrating on what employers are doing, the motivation behind their action, and the benefits gained/costs incurred are few and far between. The literature has tended to concentrate on the perspective of the individual employee, with very little empirical research on the demand side of the equation. Furthermore, much of what has been written in this area is anecdotal or in the form of case-studies, making it extremely difficult to paint an overall picture.

There are two main exceptions to this pattern.

The first, and perhaps the most comprehensive recent employer survey, was that undertaken by the Rehabilitation Resource Centre (RRC) at City University as part of their Disability Management at Work programme *(Smith, et al. 1991)*. The survey contacted 1,026 employers by postal questionnaires from which 492 replies were received, 30 per cent (146) from the private sector and 70 per cent (346) from the public sector. The survey collected information about the actions currently being taken or planned by British employers to improve employment opportunities for people with disabilities.

The second major survey was carried out by the IFF on behalf of the Employment Department in 1989 *(Morrell, 1990)*. The project undertook 1,160 detailed personal interviews from a sample of employers with 20 or more employees, chosen to be representative of the national employment profile. This was based on establishment rather than organisation. The purpose of the survey however, was not to look specifically at what employers were doing for people with disabilities, but rather to examine: firstly employers' views on the duty to employ people with disabilities through the Quota scheme; and secondly the role of the Disablement Advisory Service (DAS). The report therefore concentrates very much in these areas *(Morrell, 1990)*.

In 1986 the Banking Insurance and Finance Union carried out a survey of employers with whom BIFU had regular dealings. The survey returns covered 38 employers and more than 319,000 staff. The detail available from this survey's published findings is extremely limited and only the most general data are useful *(BIFU, 1987)*.

At a local level, there have been studies undertaken by Training and Enterprise Councils and other bodies. Sussex TEC, for example, funded a research project by their local PACT[14] into employment and the labour market as it affects people with disabilities. This project involved a survey of 392 employers, of which 91 responded, across all sectors of employment in East and West Sussex. As with the BIFU study, the data provided in the report are rather limited, and there is a heavy bias to the service sector. There is some evidence in the survey findings on the numbers of disabled persons employed, the occupations they are employed in, employer contact with support agencies, and requirements for assistance in employing people with disabilities. Nevertheless, the local nature of the survey, coupled with the low (23 per cent) response rate, caution against drawing any general conclusions from such work *(Simpson, 1992)*.

4.2 Numbers of employers employing people with disabilities

The surveys described above give some indication of the extent to which employers employ people with disabilities. The RRC survey had a fairly high proportion of employers employing people with disabilities, 486 out of 492 employers. The survey sample had included organisations known by the research team to be actively involved in action to improve employment opportunities and this may well affect how representative the results are of employers in general. The low overall response rate also raises questions of bias towards respondents with positive attitudes towards people with disabilities *(Smith et al., 1991)*.

The IFF survey results were less positive, finding that 42 per cent of responding establishments employed no people with disabilities and that 75 per cent had no registered disabled employees. Only nine per cent of establishments had registered disabled people representing three per cent or more of the workforce, although around 33 per cent employed three per cent or more people with disabilities who where not necessarily registered *(Morrell, 1990)*.

---

[14] Placing, Assessment and Counselling Team. These are set up at a local level by the Employment Service, drawing together a team of people who are skilled and experienced in helping people with disabilities in and into work, and replacing the diverse previous services operated by the Employment Service for people with disabilities.

The BIFU study found that among the staff covered there were only 1,349 registered disabled (0.4 per cent of the total). Only five employers had records of unregistered disabled employees, which added a further 1,624 to the total. These five returns covered a total labour force of 230,000 — a large proportion of those surveyed. Nevertheless even when all disabled staff are taken into account, the proportion of disabled employed was still well short of the three per cent quota at 1.1 per cent (*BIFU, 1987*).

In the Sussex area study, around 20 per cent of employers employed no people with disabilities and 30 per cent had no registered disabled employees. Of those who did employ people with disabilities, the majority had fewer than five such employees (*Simpson, 1992*).

4.3 Profile of employers employing people with disabilities

Both the RRC and IFF studies gathered information regarding the numbers and characteristics of the employers employing people with disabilities, the latter being the more detailed.

Table 8. Establishments with employees with disabilities by business activity

	Total in sample	Employers with people with disabilities	% of Total
Minerals/chemicals	40	33	82.5
Mechanical engineering	37	27	73.0
Electrical engineering	29	21	72.4
Metal goods	32	27	84.4
Textiles/clothing	29	20	69.0
Other process	81	67	82.7
Construction	54	46	85.2
Private transport	63	38	60.3
Wholesale	83	41	49.4
Financial services	119	68	57.1
Retail	153	67	43.8
Consumer services	217	104	48.0
Health	34	12	35.3
Central Government	22	8	36.4
Local Government	47	43	91.5
Education	113	26	23.0

Source: Smith et al., 1991

The IFF survey reported data regarding main business activity. Table 8 indicates the number of employers in the sample for each sector listed, the number of those employers who actually employed any people with disabilities whether registered or not and the percentage of the total they represent. From this it would seem that the Education sector is the poorest performer with only 23 per cent of establishments interviewed having any disabled employees. At the other extreme, Local Government had the highest density of establishments (91 per cent) employing people with disabilities. These figures do not however give any indication of what percentage of their workforce people with disabilities represent.

An analysis by size of these data from the IFF survey produced predictable results (Table 9). Small employers are less likely to employ disabled people than are large employees. 38.5 per cent of establishments with fewer than 20 employees employed people with disabilities, whereas for establishments employing over 100 employees the figure was over 80 per cent. Again the results do not provide any indication of what percentage of the workforce people with disabilities represent.

Table 9. Establishments with employees with disabilities by size band — IFF Survey

	Total in sample	Employers with people with disabilities	% of Total
1 — 19	26	10	38.5
20 — 49	712	318	44.7
50 — 99	229	165	72.1
100 — 199	106	85	80.2
200 — 499	56	48	85.7
500 — 999	15	12	80.0
1000 or more	9	8	88.9
Don't know	1	1	100.0

Source: Morrell, 1990

In the RRC study, only three size bands were used (1 to 1,000, 1,001 to 5,000 and 5,001 and over). Employers were asked whether they employed people with disabilities as far as they knew. Of the six employers not employing people with disabilities, five were in the smallest band and one in the 1,001 to 5,000.

A key problem with these results, is that although it appears as if the majority of employers from both surveys are employing people with disabilities, there is no indication of how many, the severity of disabilities involved, extent of the provision made to employ them or its effectiveness. Neither is there any indication of the likely severity of any response bias.

Table 10. Establishments with employees with disabilities by size band — RRC Survey

Number of employees	Private sector		Public Sector	
	Employing people with disabilities	**Not employing people with disabilities**	**Employing people with disabilities**	**Not employing people with disabilities**
1 to 1000	33	3	120	2
1001 to 5000	38	–	95	1
5001 and over	70	–	116	–
size not given	3	–	11	–
Total	144	3	342	3

Source: Smith et al., 1991

4.4 Provisions implemented

Survey findings

The surveys mentioned above provide little analysis of the response to the questions on recruitment and retention practices. The RRC survey asked employers to indicate from a list which actions they had taken, which they had planned and which were for future consideration, with the specific aim of improving employment opportunities for people with disabilities. The results are set out in Table 11 below.

Although the data give some indication of the types of initiatives employers are prepared to consider, it must be borne in mind that the question included actions planned or under future consideration as well as actually undertaken. This could well have added a spurious positive slant to the overall results.

The survey also asked organisations the number of actions they had undertaken. They found that 17 of the organisations were not undertaking any of the listed actions while 60 were involved in all eleven. Half of the organisations had undertaken six or fewer. Those taking no action were split equally between the public and private sectors. However, with only one exception, every action listed was being undertaken by a higher proportion of public sector than private sector employers. In addition the survey found a positive relationship between size of organisation and the number of actions undertaken to improve opportunities for people with disabilities.

The results from the RRC survey do not give any indication of key aspects of employer behaviour which are central to the current study, notably: the extent of the provision or its success; the motivation behind the actions; whether they were to help existing staff or improve opportunities on a wider basis; or whether the decisions

Institute of Manpower Studies

Table 11. Types of action taken, planned or for further consideration

	Sector		
Action Taken	**Private %**	**Public %**	**All %**
Had contact with DAS	83	91	90
Provided special equipment	63	70	68
Adapted premises	66	69	68
Contacted disability organisations	66	64	65
Reviewed personnel policies and practices	58	62	60
Improved recruitment	45	61	56
Consulted trade union or staff representative	39	62	56
Designated staff responsible for disability issues	45	59	55
Consulted staff with disabilities	50	55	54
Developed a disability policy	47	54	52
Reviewed training	30	34	33
Other	11	12	12

Source: Smith et al., 1991

were being made at a corporate level or by pro-active local managers. As indicated earlier, although it is encouraging to note that half of the participating organisations were making provisions for people with disabilities, the RRC itself admits that 'this is not altogether unexpected as the sample included employers known to be actively involved in this area' (*Smith et al.,1991*).

The IFF survey gathered more detailed information but mainly presented this data broken down by employers who had been visited by DAS and those who had not. For detailed views of employer provisions, the anecdotal case study material is more useful and is relied on in the following sections where provisions made by employers are studied in more detail[15].

Case studies

The RRC survey was followed up with in-depth case studies of seven organisations. Those chosen were respondents to the survey who were undertaking a variety of initiatives. These were selected to reflect the survey finding that a greater amount of activity is being carried out in the public sector than in the private sector. The case study organisations were three local authorities, a health authority, a civil service department and two private sector financial institutions (*Pilling et al., 1992*).

---

[15] This review of case study material does not purport to be comprehensive, although we have reviewed all the major UK publication sources likely to contain such material. Rather, in the lack of comprehensive survey findings on many of these issues, it should be seen as illustrative of the kind of material available.

A second report using case studies is that by RADAR (*Erne, 1991*) on the results of an employment project under the Department of Employment Pilot Employment Initiative for Disabled People (PEIDP). This was designed to increase the employment opportunities of people with disabilities, particularly through improved communication between the different services to form a coherent network. A mixture of six authorities was selected to include County Councils, District Councils, a Metropolitan Authority and a London Borough with an equal number of Conservative and Labour Councils.

Beyond these two projects, there are few systematic surveys containing a range of case studies, although there exist many single case studies which have been written up in a more anecdotal fashion — in the UK literature at least, these are heavily dominated by public sector examples.

In the rest of this chapter, then, we examine the range of findings on various aspects of employer policy and behaviour, drawing as appropriate on survey and case study material uncovered during the literature review. It should be re-emphasised, however, that this material is very patchy, and does not provide the kind of systematic, coherent overview of employer attitudes which is one of the objectives of the present study. It does, however, provide a number of insights and examples, which may be useful in developing hypotheses for further work.

4.4.1 Policy

Formal policy

The first action suggested by the Code of Good Practice is that the employer should develop a formal policy regarding the employment of people with disabilities. This is actually a legal requirement for all employers employing over 250 staff under the Companies Act of 1985.

The RRC survey found that 52 per cent of all organisations claimed that developing a disability policy was a provision undertaken, planned or considered (*Smith et al., 1991*).

The IFF study found that only 21 per cent of establishments actually had any formal written policy. When asked what had encouraged them to develop a policy, many respondents were unable to recall the original motivations. A high proportion of those who could remember, thought they were legally obliged to do so. As far as policy implementation was concerned, 65 per cent of respondents claimed that the policy was being implemented completely, with 12 per cent feeling it was implemented to some extent and 23 per cent not knowing. When asked how they ensured the policy was being implemented, between one third and one quarter of respondents were unable to give an answer (*Morrell, 1990*).

Employers with no policy

The IFF survey also looked at the attitudes of employers who had no written policy. Most stated that applications would be considered on merit. Three quarters said they would not discriminate and generally respondents fell into neither the extremely positive nor the extremely negative categories of attitudes towards employing people with disabilities. Thirteen per cent said they would recruit people with disabilities only to certain jobs and six per cent said they would not be considered at all. With regard to the attitudes of line managers and employees, 44 per cent of line managers were very willing to have people with disabilities as part of their team, with 41 per cent being fairly willing. Forty nine per cent of employees had a very positive attitude to working with people with disabilities and 44 per cent were fairly positive.

Disability officers

In addition to having a policy regarding people with disabilities, some organisations have found the appointment of a manager to implement the policy essential to its success. Fifty five per cent of respondents to the RRC study had designated or planned to designate someone responsible for disability issues.

National Westminster Bank, in January 1987, appointed a full-time manager to look after this area. Since the new manager had been appointed the number of people with disabilities employed by the bank rose from 1,216 to 1,391, of whom 361 are registered disabled, out of a total workforce of 88,000 (*IRS, 1990*).

A recent report by the Employment Service's Research and Evaluation Branch (*Taylor, 1990*) on local authority attitudes to the Sheltered Placement Scheme (SPS) concluded that the key factor important in the success of an authority's attempt to use the SPS scheme is the appointment of an officer whose sole responsibility is the management of the project.

4.4.2 Attracting job applicants with disabilities

Designating jobs for disabled only

One of the most stringent employment policies implemented was that of the *London Borough of Lambeth* in 1986. Prior to 1986 the Council had always successfully applied for a permit and as a result disabled employees represented one per cent of the workforce. In 1986 they decided not to apply for a permit and to fulfil their three per cent quota. This meant they could only recruit registered disabled people until this three per cent target was reached (*Gledhill, 1989*). The council found it had to completely change the copy and format of their advertising. All job advertisements carried the statement 'only people who are registered disabled will be appointed to this job'. The advert also encouraged non-registered applicants as long as the person agreed to register if they took the job. The policy ran for two and a half months after which time jobs that had received no suitable applicants were opened to able-bodied as well. Although there were some difficulties with this approach, which will be discussed in a later section, the policy was generally a success. Within six months the three per cent target had been reached. The number of registered disabled employees rose from 90 to 340.

The *London Borough of Hackney* adopted a similar policy to that of Lambeth. From June to October 1989 the council reserved 100 jobs for disabled people across most departments. Only people with disabilities could apply. Prior to this initiative, Hackney had 44 names on a contact vacancy list. After a publicity statement was distributed outlining the scheme this rose to 350. A total of 30 people were employed as a result of the campaign (*Erne, 1991*).

Nottingham County Council introduced a system of designating five per cent of the weekly Council vacancies to people with disabilities, some of which are advertised for people with disabilities only. If after the closing date a suitable candidate has not been found, the job is opened to everyone (*Pilling, 1992*).

Advertising

Many local authorities and organisations now use specifically worded job advertisements to encourage applications from people with disabilities, for example *Hampshire County Council* (*Erne, 1991*). This, however, is not the only option used to raise the number of applicants from people with disabilities. Often posts will be advertised in disability publications, as in the *Parkside Health Authority Scheme* (1990), *Sheffield City Council* and at the *London Borough of Wandsworth* (*Erne, 1991*) whilst some organisations, for example *Hull City Council, Cheshire County Counci* (*Erne, 1991*) and *Anglia Television (IDS, 1992)* send all job details to the local job centres, DROs and to DAS. *Kent County Council* arranged an interview with their Chief Personnel Officer on local radio in order to publicise their policy which resulted in 30 enquiries (*Erne, 1991*).

Developing links with voluntary bodies

One very important avenue for attracting applicants is through developing links with voluntary organisations. Sixty five per cent of respondents to the RRC survey claimed to have contacted disability organisations with this end in mind, and examples from case studies include *London Electricity Board* (*Employment Gazette, 1990*), *Parkside Health Authority (1990), Cheshire County Council* (*Erne, 1991*), *Anglia Television* (*IDS, 1992*) and *Canadian National* (the national railway company) in Canada. In the latter case, CN established an outreach programme, making contacts with organisations that help people with disabilities and giving them information about job opportunities in the company. In Toronto, the recruitment manager faxes details of job openings to 75 local organisations. (*PM Plus, 1992*).

When the *McDonald's* fast food chain began its McJobs programme to recruit, train and retain individuals with disabilities, the programme manager met with most state departments of vocational rehabilitation (VR) in order to promote the scheme. The McJobs coaches now work closely with the local VR centre to identify potential trainees (*Laabs*, *1991*).

Open days/employment fairs

In order to publicise the opportunities available and advertise vacancies to people with disabilities, targeted events or open days may prove useful. The Parkside scheme arranged a half day careers advice session for people with disabilities using a disability organisation's premises. This meant that all the necessary facilities such as parking and accessible premises were available. In order to ensure access to information a sign language interpreter was made available and a general information pack was produced on tape. Other local authorities have attended similar employment fairs organised by local disability organisations. *Hampshire County Council* and Portsmouth Handicap Action Committee received many enquiries after taking part in an Employment Fair organised with Portsmouth City Council (*Erne, 1991*).

Other advice to potential applicants

Hampshire County Council produced a leaflet offering advice on filling in application forms and explaining the reasons for the questions on disability in order to make people with disabilities more at ease with applying for jobs (*Erne, 1991*).

4.4.3 Job descriptions

Using advertisements with statements such as 'Applications from people with disabilities are particularly welcome' is not enough to encourage disabled candidates. Despite assurances such as this, job descriptions and requirements will often put off a candidate with a disability from applying. The Code of Good Practice points out that in many cases requirements listed for the job may well not be essential and could form a barrier to people with disabilities. The IFF survey found that many job requirements were far too tightly drawn. They quote the example that 41 per cent of management jobs were perceived to require the ability to walk over half a mile whilst 23 per cent were required to lift heavy weights (*Morrell, 1990*).

In Canada where legislation to support people with disabilities has been in place for five years, *Canadian National* have reviewed all employment policies and procedures. They have subsequently removed all blanket exclusions to jobs to overcome the problem of unnecessary requirements. They have attempted to dismiss the assumption that certain types of people are unable to do certain types of work. They assess each candidate individually, measuring their ability to do the job (*PM Plus, 1992*).

Some Local Authorities also have policy statements regarding flexible job requirements. For example *Cheshire County Council* states that 'where necessary, the Council will call upon expert medical, psychological or technical advice to help assess whether a job is, or can be made suitable for a particular handicapped person, to identify a training need or consider adaptations to a workplace or methods to make a job more suitable for a particular handicap' (*Erne, 1991*).

4.4.4 Modifying recruitment and selection procedures

Once individuals have been persuaded to apply for a job, recruitment and selection procedures provide an equal chance for people with disabilities. A recent study by the Spastics Society (*Graham, Jordan & Lamb, 1990*) found that people with disabilities faced unjustifiable discrimination in the labour market. This was measured by looking at employers' responses to two fictitious applications for secretarial jobs which differed only in that one was from a disabled candidate and the other was not. 197 applications were sent out which received 147 replies to both applicants. Of the 94 employers showing a positive interest in at least one of the applicants, 88 employers were interested in the application from the able bodied candidate and only 57 in the disabled applicant. In six cases the able-bodied candidate was rejected, whilst 37 employers rejected the disabled candidate. The able-bodied candidate received 1.5 times more positive offers.

Guaranteed interview scheme

In order to overcome such problems, several organisations have altered their recruitment and selection procedures. Following the Code of Good Practice many organisations have introduced a guaranteed interview scheme to ensure that candidates who meet the basic requirements for the job are automatically offered an interview, to allow candidates to demonstrate their ability. Examples include *Anglia Television (IDS, 1992)*, *London Electricity Board (Employment Gazette, 1990)*, *Parkside Health Authority (1992)*, *Lancashire County Council* and all six organisations participating in the RADAR PEIDP scheme (*Erne, 1991*). Similarly *Birmingham City Council* decided that no job applicant would be rejected for reasons such as inaccessible premises or because of a disability which is unrelated to the job description (*IRS, 1990*).

Interview process

Ensuring that individuals get a fair interview is a central part of ensuring equal opportunities.

Parkside Health Authority (1992), in letters of invitation for interview, ask candidates if any special arrangements need to be made. This is important in helping the individual feel more at ease. They also arrange for voluntary organisations to give personnel officers training sessions on interviewing people with disabilities as well as visiting the health authority to identify and offer advice on overcoming any problems they may encounter.

Similarly, the *Royal Mail* in Merseyside used the Merseyside Society for the Deaf to evolve a format for interviewing deaf candidates whom they were particularly aiming to recruit (*Fewster, 1991*).

Several of the Local Authorities in the RADAR project used DAS to train their personnel staff in interviewing techniques as well as other personnel aspects (*Erne, 1991; Pilling, 1992*).

Royal Mail, although wishing to treat deaf applicants in the same way as hearing applicants, recognised the need to allow them more time for interpreting. Poor lighting, slurred or rapid speech or a regional accent were avoided. They also made provision for applicants to chat with existing deaf employees since this was likely to set them more at ease (*Fewster, 1991*).

In Canada, *Canadian National* found that commercially produced tests had to be replaced with task-based tests developed by occupational psychologists specifically for CN. Efforts are also made to ensure that the way these tests are administered does not discriminate against people with disabilities. For example text of a written test was enlarged to accommodate a visually impaired candidate, whilst test instructions were given in sign language for the benefit of a deaf candidate (*PM Plus, 1992*).

Registers of applicants

In the Parkside scheme unsuccessful candidates at shortlisting/ selection stages were offered counselling whilst unsuccessful applicants were kept on file for future vacancies. This was a common policy throughout many of the Local Authorities studied (*Erne, 1991; Pilling, 1992*). Often an organisation will develop a register of individuals with disabilities who are available for work. *Nottingham County Council* has devised a computer system to match data relating to applicants as well as data relating to vacant positions within the Council (*Pilling, 1992*).

Hewlett-Packard applies the same recruitment process to applicants with disabilities as for other candidates, but should the applicant not be suitable for the vacancy or has applied speculatively, they are asked to attend an informal interview. A staffing specialist during the interview will assess the individual about the type of work he or she can do and their details are held on file in the event that a suitable vacancy occurs (*IDS, 1992*).

4.5 Work experience and training schemes

Involvement in work experience or training schemes for people with disabilities may also be a mechanism through which subsequent recruitment can occur, as well as an important contribution to helping people with disabilities gain access to the labour market. Thus, for example, *Parkside Health Authority (1992)* offered work experience placements to disabled candidates who were unsuccessful at interview and people who had made enquiries at times when there were no vacancies. Training organisations dealing with people with disabilities were also contacted to offer them placements.

Birmingham City Council finances and operates a 'supernumerary' Scheme, whereby people with disabilities can gain real work experience on a trial basis. This is currently placing its fourth intake of 'students'. So far it has been very successful with more than 90 per cent of participants now placed in permanent employment. Several of the other local authorities also provided work experience for both school leavers and the unemployed (*Erne, 1991; Pilling, 1992*).

The *McDonald's* McJobs scheme involves a six to eight week training programme with a local job coach in which individuals learn specific job skills, firstly in the class room and then on-site enabling them to integrate gradually into the work environment. Over 90 per cent complete the training and since 1981 more than 9,000 people with disabilities have been recruited through the scheme (*Laabs, 1991*).

Taking this a degree further, the American fast food chain *Frisch's* became involved in a high school project for disabled teenagers. The schools were running a new course for students with disabilities. In order to provide the facilities for students to learn catering skills in replica, Frisch built on site restaurants and contributed the raw materials. After two years of training most students hope to get jobs with Frisch (*PM Plus, 1991*).

The *Spastics Society* in the UK has set up the first fast track management development programme for disabled graduates. Although the Society employs just over three per cent from people with disabilities, there has never been a disabled person in a senior management job. They now have nine graduates on the three year course (*Martin, 1991*).

London Fancy Box (LFB) is a company producing rigid cardboard presentation boxes at three factories in Dover. It had always applied for a permit on the grounds that it never received enough suitable applications from people with disabilities. In 1982 the company decided that this was not acceptable and has subsequently recruited two or three young people with special needs onto their training programme each year. This provided certificated qualifications for all employees. Staff with management potential attend block release courses at the London College of Printing. Others took City and Guilds courses in basic engineering at a local college. In addition to this scheme, if the employer was not sure if a person with a disability would be able to cope with employment or training they would be taken on using the ES Job Introduction Scheme whereby ED pay £45 the wages for a trial period of six weeks which can be extended for a further seven weeks. If after this the individual is not able to proceed, they are transferred if possible to sheltered placement (*IRS, 1990*).

4.6 Monitoring new and existing staff

Obtaining information on staff with a disability is a very common problem with many organisations. The problems fall into two main areas: identifying existing staff and gathering information on new recruits.

Identifying existing staff

As indicated by earlier surveys, many personnel departments may not be aware of people with disabilities within their organisation because they are not registered disabled. In the IFF survey, for example, just over three-quarters of employers were very or fairly confident that, under their definition of disability, they knew the number of employees with disabilities within their establishment. The reasons given for not knowing were generally due to the individual concealing a disability because of the perceived stigma involved, or that it was felt not directly to affect their work. There were also employers who said that they had not been told of employees becoming disabled. The levels of claimed record-keeping were however fairly low, particularly where unregistered people with disabilities were concerned (*Morrell, 1990*). This finding was supported by the RRC report which found that 95 per cent of private sector and 96 per cent of public sector organisations had a system for recording registered disabled employees but only 29 per cent of private sector and 26 per cent of public sector organisations had a system to cover those who were not registered.

The *Parkside Health Authority* had no records of non-registered staff with disabilities. Questions were therefore included in workforce headcounts to obtain an idea of those disabled but not registered. This required updating of the personnel computer system (*1992*).

National Westminster Bank made its first priority to establish a database of information on existing staff with disabilities, the work they were doing and the equipment the organisation already possessed which could help such individuals function as effectively as other staff. This information was helpful in enabling the manager to disseminate good practice in, for example, one region to all the other regions (*IRS, 1990*). There are several similar examples in the public sector of such schemes (*Erne, 1991; Pilling, 1992*).

Both *Midland Bank* and *Boots* are running pilot schemes into monitoring staff. Both have found the area has had to be approached very sensitively. Midland has attempted to build awareness of its monitoring process for six months before starting the pilot. Boots will only send out their questionnaires after it has been discussed with the local DAS. Central to the success of monitoring is assuring staff that information will be treated confidentially and that there is a commitment from employers to use the information to develop sound practices (*Morgan, 1992*).

New employees

Traditionally, disability has been viewed as a private concern in many employing organisations, but views have changed and several case-studies show organisations altering application forms to include questions of disability whether individuals are registered or not. Again, individuals typically have to be encouraged to give the information and hence *Hampshire County Council*, for example, sends out leaflets explaining the application form to all applicants (*Erne, 1991*).

This policy does not apply to the public sector only. The *Alliance and Leicester Building Society*, for example, now asks applicants:

'Have you a disability which you would like us to know about? If so, is there any special help you would like us to provide for you to do this job?' (*Pilling, 1992*).

Parkside Health Authority (1992) found that its computerised personnel system for new employees was inadequate, since it only covered people who were registered as disabled. Hence they decided to redesign application forms to ask whether the applicant considered her/himself to be disabled.

Once information is gathered on both existing staff and new recruits, it is essential that a system is developed such that the data can be used to ensure that any targets are being met. Several organisations use the information to develop action plans and guidelines to managers on what it is possible to do (*Erne, 1991; Pilling, 1992*).

4.7 People with disabilities at work

4.7.1 Flexibility

Once in work, a disabled individual's progress should be monitored, as with any new recruit, and changes in provision and work organisation made if necessary. In the *Frisch's* restaurants they found flexibility and accommodation were essential aspects of employing people with disabilities. An example is given of a person employed to wash dishes who proved who unable to keep up with the fast pace at lunch time. The company hired another dishwasher to help, with one working mornings, one working afternoons and overlapping at lunchtime to cover the extra work. 'If someone can fulfil 80 per cent of a job, we can find someone else to do the other 20 per cent'. They found that appropriate accommodations could be as simple as providing a stool for someone who could not stand for long periods (*PM Plus, 1991*).

Birmingham City Council introduced a range of schemes such as job sharing and flexible working hours, which although arguably benefitting all employees, were seen as being of particular help to people with disabilities (*Pilling, 1992*). Others such as the *London Electricity Board*, have allowed the option for disabled employees of working from home where appropriate (*Employment Gazette, 1990*).

4.7.2 Staff support

Frisch's managers used rehabilitation agencies to train existing staff in coaching and support for new employees with disabilities. Managers were given a matrix listing telephone numbers and contact names of all the agencies and advice on which types of job were most suited for people with which type of disability (*PM Plus, 1991*).

Parkside Health Authority (1992) developed a support group for disabled staff. The purpose was to enable disabled employees to work together in tackling obstacles. This initiative led to a focus on career development for disabled staff resulting in two specialist courses. What became clear in Parkside's case was the need to provide positive support, for instance in terms of making time/resources available.

4.7.3 Health and safety

One of the main areas of concern for employers over people with disabilities is that of health and safety. Such concerns often prove to be unjustified. The *Royal Mail* in Merseyside for example had considered, with the financial help of the Employment Service fitting flashing lights to fire alarms. It was also planned to designate certain members of staff as responsible for letting deaf staff know in case of an emergency. In practice deaf people simply followed other staff when the drill sounded (*Fewsher, 1991*). Similar procedures have been adopted by *LEB (IDS, 1992)*.

Birmingham City Council has developed a Code of Practice which covers emergency and evacuation and health and safety of people with disabilities, which states that an appropriate evacuation procedure must be worked out in case of emergency, and training given in its use. Various adaptations have been made for individual employees, such as a flashing light emergency alarm for a deaf employee (*Pilling, 1992*).

Other examples of emergency equipment include the purchase by *London Borough of Wandsworth* of PARAID evac-chairs to assist disabled people out of buildings in case of an emergency (*Erne, 1991*).

4.7.4 Training

Only 12 per cent of respondents to the RRC study had planned or reviewed training in the light of the needs of people with disabilities (*Smith et al., 1991*). This is an important area of possible oversight on the part of employers. Without equal chances to training, individuals with disabilities may not have equal opportunities for promotion. Changes may involve simply ensuring that all training courses are run at centres with access for disabilities.

Birmingham City Council, for example, has its own residential training centre and to fulfil its commitment to people with disabilities, ramps have been installed and study bedrooms are available with a specially adapted bathroom en suite (*IRS, 1990*).

Anglia Television, whilst building a new training room, considered making it user-friendly for people with disabilities by installing, for example, an induction loop (*IDS, 1992*).

Hampshire County Council were reported to be exploring the feasibility of setting places aside for people with disabilities on training schemes within the Council (*Erne, 1991*).

It may, however, be necessary to develop special courses or to restructure courses so they are relevant or accessible to people with disabilities. *National Westminster Bank*, for example has run an experimental in-house word processing course for visually handicapped secretaries. *Birmingham City Council* developed a career development training course for employees with disabilities. These were used to identify areas of general concern and individual needs for training. The issues which emerge from these courses are used by management to promote change at an individual level (*Pilling, 1992*).

4.7.5 Promotion

There is little evidence on policies and practices which relate to the promotion of people with disabilities. This issue was, however, considered in the RADAR study of local authority practice, suggesting that as in the cases of training and retention, most authorities had a policy on promotion which typically stated that the authority would give full and fair consideration to applications for promotion from disabled people. There is, however, little evidence to suggest how such provisions are implemented (*Erne, 1991*).

4.8 Retaining staff who become disabled

There is very little evidence from previous studies or reports on employer policy and practice towards existing staff who become disabled.

Clearly, many of the actions cited in the paragraphs above will naturally also apply to retaining staff who have become disabled. Again flexibility and accommodation are the key words. Several reports on individual organisations however (*eg* Parkside Health Authority) have suggested that employers have found it more difficult to make progress in developing explicit policy in this area than on recruitment and selection. Initially *Parkside Health Authority*, for example, drew up a policy on retaining staff. This included a section on re-employment whereby an individual becoming disabled would be considered for suitable vacancies when they arose. It was argued, however, that it would be useful to look at some of the retention initiatives geared towards gender equality (*eg* Opportunity 2000 on retention of nurses) to see whether these could be expanded to cover disabled staff (*1992*).

Most local authorities covered in the RADAR study had some sort of policy statement on retaining staff becoming disabled. *Cheshire County Council's* policy includes provision for people to be redeployed to other areas of work where their salaries would be protected and their abilities maximised. The policy was under review to ensure it was fully implemented (*Erne ,1991*).

4.9 Raising awareness among all employees

The RRC survey found that 56 per cent of respondents had consulted trade union or staff representatives in their attempt to improve opportunities for people with disabilities (*Smith et al., 1991*). The subsequent case study work provided numerous examples of different staff awareness schemes implemented. The schemes varied according to whether they were aimed at personnel staff only, management and supervisors, or to encompass all employees.

More generally, the case-studies available in the personnel and industrial relations literature suggest that the importance of training and awareness for existing staff is a message that has got through to those employers who are involved in disability initiatives.

National Westminster's manager for disabled staff was reported as seeing one of her future tasks as encouraging managers to focus on the abilities of all staff. A video was prepared which was to be shown to all employees with personnel or equal opportunities responsibilities. It was hoped that by demonstrating the range of talents contributed to the organisation by staff with an occupational handicap all employees will be encouraged to take a more positive attitude to employing people with disabilities (*IRS, 1990*).

When *Frisch's* decided to introduce a programme for people with disabilities, the company's management recruiter organised a two-day seminar with 60 rehabilitation agencies for all area managers, unit managers and their assistants. The agencies explained what would help them, while the managers outlined their worries about employing disabled people. Similarly, in order to make managers at *Canadian National* more receptive to the idea of employing people with disabilities, all 3,000 of their first-line supervisors received training on managing a diverse workforce. As well as raising their awareness of diversity of issues, this one-day workshop is intended to give supervisors some knowledge of the relevant legislation. They found that once made aware of their own responsibilities, supervisors were usually able to find creative solutions to the every day problems involved in managing a diverse workforce (*PM Plus, 1992*).

Royal Mail sent its managers on training sessions run by the Merseyside Society for the Deaf on how it felt to be deaf, what aids were available, and role plays tailored to the company (*Fewsher, 1991*). Similarly, *LEB* and *McDonalds* (*Laabs, 1991*) have developed training to promote understanding of disability among staff and managers (*Employment Gazette, 1990; IDS, 1992*).

Lambeth Council felt that one of the failings of their initiative to increase the employment of people with disabilities, had been that many managers in personnel felt that they had been thrown in at the deep end and that training into the implications of employing people with disabilities would have proved invaluable (*Gledhill, 1989*).

A major focus of the *Parkside Health Authority* (1992) initiative in the first stages was on raising the level of knowledge and awareness amongst personnel officers. Further short awareness sessions were run for managers. Overall, the training to raise awareness had two separate emphases: one focusing on the services available, such as grants for adaption of premises and equipment; the second on identifying and challenging attitudes.

Cheshire County Council used disability awareness training in their interviewing and selection courses provided by the DAS. A training course was also held for trainers which included a session on simulating disability. More generally, disability awareness training courses for managers arranged by DAS were taken up by several local authorities, reported in the RADAR study (*Erne, 1991*). In order to raise awareness among all staff Cheshire produced a series of pamphlets on specific disabilities similar to those produced by the Employment Service. They were in the format of its disability policy, in user-friendly language and with the Cheshire contact addresses (*Erne, 1991*).

4.10 Access and special equipment

The RRC survey in the UK, found provision of special equipment and adapting premises were the second most commonly cited actions which had been undertaken, planned or considered by employers — 68 per cent responding positively to these questions (the commonest was making contact with the DAS) (*Smith et al., 1991*).

Whilst some studies cite employer concern about the costs of making such provision for employees with disabilities, there is no systematic evidence for the UK on how much employers actually spend on equipment, adaptations for the disabled *etc*. Studies in the US, however, have found that many adaptations and special equipment to facilitate the employment of people with disabilities are simple and inexpensive. A study quoted in the *US Equal Employment Opportunity Commission* paper (*1991*) found that most frequently cited accommodations accounting for 51.1 per cent of those undertaken were made at no cost, 18.5 per cent at costs between $1 and $99, and 11.9 per cent at costs between $100 and $499. Thus more than 80 per cent of all accommodations cost less than $500. Another study by the disabilities product information service found that of the most commonly needed adaptations for computer equipment and software, 69 per cent cost less than $500 (*Snell, 1992*).

Adapting new premises

The relatively low costs of making such physical accommodations were confirmed in a case study of the *TSB Group*. When the group planned to move its head offices, it was decided as part of the refurbishment plans that the new building was to be fully accessible for people with disabilities. Entrances to the building do not have steps so they are accessible to wheel-chair users. There are taped announcements in lifts, induction loops in conference areas, light reflecting carpets and wall paper, floor surface changes at strategic points, large print signs and tactile maps to enhance navigation about the building. The design specification was drawn up in consultation with the RNID, RNIB and the Centre for Accessible Environments. The costs for this were regarded as being minimal in comparison with those being incurred through the general refurbishment (*Pilling, 1992*).

Hewlett-Packard's current Bristol site was purpose built in 1984 to take into account the needs of people with disabilities. The entire site is built on one level, open plan with wide corridors and doors, ramps into the building, disabled toilets and disabled parking facilities (*IDS, 1992*).

Adapting existing premises

Other employers have taken on such changes without moving. To ensure that people with disabilities are able to work once they have been selected, *Canadian National* carried out an accommodation study of all its buildings and set up a $10,000 contingency fund for managers wanting to accommodate people with disabilities but not having sufficient funds in their operating budgets (*PM Plus, 1992*).

In the UK, *Leicestershire County Council* established a capital programme of improvements in access to Council building and buildings in which the Council operates an agency agreement (*Erne, 1991*)

Anglia Television, despite difficulties of being situated in historic buildings, has over the past two and a half years allocated funds for adaptations such as installing ramps, designating lifts for use of people with disabilities and providing disabled toilets (*IDS, 1992*).

Use of special equipment

As well as special equipment mentioned earlier to enhance health and safety procedures, there is a wide range of equipment which can be used to accommodate people with disabilities, and some of the case study literature exemplifies employer introduction of such equipment.

National Westminster's own IT systems development department in 1990 provided most of the micro-computing equipment required by disabled staff. Many others buy in equipment and computer software from outside which is, as indicated earlier, often inexpensive (*Snell, 1992*).

The BIFU survey found that out of 22 replies to the question on special equipment, 11 employers stated that they had specific facilities for disabled staff including talking calculators, braille typewriters, Sinclair work station, CC TV appliances, switchboard with synthetic speech, Optacon document readers and modified VDU screens (*BIFU, 1987*).

5. Employer Motivation for Disability Policies and Practices

A key focus of the proposed study is to examine not only *what* actions employers do or do not undertake with regard to recruiting and employing people with disabilities, but also to investigate what motivates them to behave in the way they do. Once again, there is little in the existing literature in the way of systematic evidence on this question. We look in turn at the key factors which are mentioned as possible influencing factors in this regard.

5.1 Legal obligation

With the possible exception of the largest organisations, it seems unlikely that the major source of employer motivation in adopting and implementing a policy on employment of people with disabilities is one of legal obligation. The evidence suggests that permits exempting employers from the quota obligations are obtained with ease, and prosecutions of those who do not obtain them despite not meeting the quota are rare.

5.2 Moral obligation

Among the majority of public sector organisations as well as many of the larger, high profile companies, a motivation to move on the disability front appears to be associated with or to emerge from a commitment to equal opportunities in general. Disability issues are commonly embodied in more wide-ranging equal opportunity policies or statements. That of *Birmingham City Council* is fairly typical, stating that the Council:

> '..will ensure that all existing and potential employees receive equal consideration and is committed to the elimination of unlawful and unfair discrimination on the grounds of gender, race, disability, colour, ethnic and national origin, nationality, sexuality, marital status, responsibility for dependants, religion, trade union activity and age' (*Pilling, 1992*).

In addition to a general commitment to equal opportunities in employment, several other motivating factors for employer disability policies emerge from the case study literature.

5.3 DAS contact

Contact by the Disability Advisory Service, raising awareness of the issues concerning disability is not infrequently cited in case studies as having influenced recruitment policy (*Pilling, 1992*). The IFF survey, in order to assess the effectiveness of DAS, compared the differing levels of activity between similar establishments which had or had not received visits from the service. The overall results are shown in Table 12 below.

Table 12. Types of action taken by DAS and non-DAS contacts

	Percentage taking any action		
	Total %	DAS %	Non-Das %
Recruitment	7	16	4
Quota Scheme	8	17	6
Positive Attitude	11	17	10
Retention	14	20	13
Policy	8	13	5
Sheltered Placement Schemes	2	10	1

Source: Morrell, 1990

The survey found that a higher proportion of employers with DAS contacts made an active effort to recruit people with disabilities than did their counterparts in the non-DAS group. This seemed irrespective of size or business activity. DAS contacts were also more likely to have made extra provision for their employees with disabilities. They were far more likely to have been involved in job re-structuring, special training, making changes to existing equipment or the provision of additional equipment and allowing more flexible or shorter working hours. They were not only more aware but much more likely to have used recruiting services available, schemes such as the Job Introduction Scheme and help with adaptations (*Morrell, 1990*). There is, of course, an important question of causality here — that is, the positive relationship between having had a DAS contact and having undertaken some kind of action on behalf of employees with disabilities, may partly reflect employers taking or being committed to take action being more likely to contact the DAS themselves, or to respond positively to a request from DAS for a visit.

5.4 Skill shortages

An emergent motivation for employer action on the disability front during the late 1980s was concern about the impact of skill shortages and the 'demographic timebomb', and the associated attempt to widen recruitment pools and make better utilisation of the existing labour force (see *Hewitson-Ratcliffe, 1990*). Such concerns (in the UK at least) have clearly been mitigated by the current recession, and it is as yet unclear how far they will re-emerge when the recovery comes.

Some case study evidence (mostly predating the recession) confirms that some employers have developed/implemented policies for people with disabilities, at least partly for such reasons.

Sun Alliance developed a policy on employing more people with disabilities because of its concern about strong competition for high calibre staff in the local area. It was felt that people with disabilities would fill the roles required (*Pilling, 1992*).

Frisch's, the US fast food chain made the decision to employ more people with disabilities after realising that they were more reliable employees than average. The company at the time was suffering from high staff turnover compounded by a shrinking market of young people. One of their more dependable sources of labour was people with disabilities. With the employment of people with disabilities, turnover dropped from 260 per cent to 230 per cent (*PM Plus, 1991*).

McDonald's developed its McJobs programme because it saw people with disabilities as the largest pool of under-utilised labour in the US and felt it could no longer leave this valuable source of employees untapped. They have found that 87 per cent of participants who graduate are retained by the company (*Laabs, 1991*).

5.5 Interest initiated as a result of already disabled staff

Some organisations which have made provision for people with disabilities have done so to retain a valued member of staff. Thus, for example, *Sun Alliance* stated that an interest in disability issues developed after the access requirements of a member of staff, who is a wheelchair user, led to adaptation to their offices. Consultations on disability issues were necessitated when it was realised that adaptations which had been made were not adequate and so stimulated further changes (*Pilling, 1992*).

Canadian National in Canada had made some considerable changes to retain a particular member of staff. Despite its costs, their belief was that they had a well-trained employee with 30 more years of work ahead of him which would have been lost had accommodations not been made. This was felt to be a far more effective solution than finding a replacement (*PM Plus, 1992*). Despite the existing Canadian legislation supporting people with disabilities, this was not cited as the reason for CN's policy, although it is likely to have been a contributory factor to the organisation's awareness of the issues and possibilities available.

5.6 Attitudes of personnel staff

The time available and enthusiasm of personnel staff have been cited as reasons for developing provision. The *Frisch's* fast food chain felt that much of their policy was as a result of a particular manager in the HR department having an interest in the subject. Similarly, in the UK, a recent report by the Employment Service's Research and Evaluation Branch (*Taylor, 1990*) on local authority attitudes to the Sheltered Placement Scheme concluded that the key factor important in the success of an authority's attempt to use the Scheme is the appointment of an officer whose sole responsibility is the management of the project.

Ironically, it has also been argued that reduction in recruitment activity due to the economic downturn, may also have freed up personnel staff from the usual direct recruitment issues to concentrate in other often neglected areas, such as practices towards disability (*Pilling, 1992*).

5.7 Financial benefits

In the United States organisations taking action on disability may also receive direct financial benefits. Companies can claim a tax credit for every employee under a government scheme for employers who provide 'target jobs' for people with disabilities. They are also able to claim grants under the Job Training Partnership Act from the local Private Industry Council (the US equivalent of a TEC/LEC) (*PM Plus, 1991*).

McDonald's receives $800 for each client it trains on its McJobs scheme, which helps offset training materials and the job coach's salary (*Laabs, 1991*).

Some of the US case study literature also cites indirect financial savings acting as a motivation to undertake actions on behalf of disabled employees. Thus, the *Principal Financial Group* in Iowa, despite managing many other companies disability payment schemes, realised in the 1980s that it had no mechanisms itself for transition of its own employees back to work following a short or long term disability. The Company realised it stood to save thousands of dollars in disability claims and in costs not incurred for replacement, training and hiring temporary staff. They subsequently developed the Mainstream Programme which has saved the company more than $1 million since its inception in 1986. From 1990 to 1991 alone the company reported savings of $774,859, the majority, $730,812 saved by reducing disability claims (*Tucker, 1992*).

No UK evidence was uncovered on this issue during the literature search.

5.8 Contact with voluntary organisations

Contact with voluntary organisation has also been an important force in the employment of people with disabilities. As with contact with DAS, these organisations are able to raise awareness. *Sun Alliance* felt that its being approached to join the Local Employers' Forum on disability had contributed to its interest (*Pilling, 1992*). Many other examples are cited where voluntary organisations have been instrumental in setting up open days, forums, seminars, training schemes *etc.* to encourage the employment of people with disabilities (*PM Plus, 1991; Martin, 1991; Erne, 1991; Pilling, 1992*).

6. Costs Incurred and Problems Encountered

6.1 Costs incurred

Information in the literature regarding the costs incurred in providing for people with disabilities is virtually non existent for organisations within the UK.

Surveys in the United States are far more prevalent due to the recent Americans with Disabilities Act. As mentioned in section 4.10 studies in the US have found that many adaptations and special equipment are often simple and inexpensive.

Case study material gives very little detail on the costs of activities undertaken. Much of it outlines policies and activities but not costs.

6.2 Problems encountered

The only survey to ask questions on problems encountered was that by the IFF. The interviewers asked about the problems which respondents felt their particular establishments faced when employing people with disabilities. The results were given for all establishments and then split between those having received DAS visits and those which had not.

Table 13. Problems faced in employing people with disabilities

	Total %	DAS %	Non-DAS %
Unsuitable job types	38	36	37
Unsuitable premises	27	27	27
Lack of disabled applicants	17	12	18
Difficult access – journey to work	5	6	5
Shiftworking	3	2	4
Other	5	5	5
No problems	39	41	39

Source: Morrell, 1990

The most important problems were unsuitable job types, unsuitable premises and lack of disabled applicants. It is not known whether these responses were based on experience of actually attempting to employ people with disabilities or whether these are just perceived problems. In order to assess any real difficulties faced through actual experience, the case study literature must be used. We summarise below some of the issues raised in the case-studies which were identified as posing problems or difficulties in this area.

Financial constraints

Even in the case study literature, however, there is very little evidence on any costs and financial burdens which disability provision does place on employers (with the exception of some of the local authority case-studies, reported in *Erne, 1991*, which stated that overall financial constraints had put limits on their implementation of desired policies and actions on disability issues).

Size of organisation

According to the Disability Initiative Officer of *Birmingham City Council* the biggest problem in instigating change in the employment of people with disabilities is the sheer size of the organisation. It was felt that it was easy to make changes in small areas but these would have no effect throughout the organisation unless they could be implemented at senior management level or politician level (*Pilling, 1992*). Strategic change can only be achieved if it is instigated at the highest level, and if central control is relinquished initiatives are likely to be side-lined. It is, however, difficult to see that this is a problem which is specific to disability policy as against any other policy area.

Lack of vacancies

This has been cited as an issue in some (mainly public sector case-studies, limiting the options for responding to the needs of existing employees who become disabled.

Thus *Dover District Counci*l had found difficulty in finding suitable alternative employment for people who had become disabled and wanted to avoid ill health retirement. Alternative employment was always investigated but with the loss of vacancies due to cut-backs and compulsory competitive tendering, it did not always prove possible (*Erne, 1991*). Compulsory competitive tendering was similarly seen as a problem by *Hampshire County Council* (*Erne, 1991*).

Parkside Health Authority found that some placement officers were asking for junior non stressful clerical positions for disabled trainees finishing office skills course. These kind of jobs no longer exist in the units (*1992*).

Lack of disabled applicants

This problem arises less often in the case-studies identified than might be expected. It would seem that when organisations embark on a programme of employing people with disabilities they will use several avenues of recruitment in order to attract as many candidates as possible, and are frequently successful in tapping into a pool of disabled applicants.

The *London Borough of Wandsworth*, however, reported a very poor response to their attempts to set up an application form bank. After issuing a publicity statement in various disability publications over a period of four months, only one individual out of eleven returned the application form. They were unsure of the reason for the poor response but assumed that either the particular jobs they were seeking or were suited to were not available at the Council, or perhaps they had found situations elsewhere (*Erne, 1991*).

Parkside Health Authority initially found that after some considerable effort to attract applicants the response was slow and this led to disappointment. It was subsequently realised that it would be necessary to maintain and build up the authority's profile since the Health Service has a poor reputation nationally as an employer of people with disabilities (1992).

This was not a problem restricted to the UK. *Canadian National* found that despite considerable efforts, they had far more success in recruiting women and members of visible minority groups than people with disabilities. In 1991 of a total of 19,169 applications only 278 were from people with disabilities. Of 647 hired only 12 had disabilities. CN believed this could be put down, in part, to the nature of their business activities — many people with certain kinds of disabilities can not work on trains whatever adjustments/ adaptations are made (*PM Plus, 1992*).

Such shortages of disabled applicants appear more pronounced for posts at higher levels of skill and qualification, and as we have seen above (Section 2.2), disabled people are generally less well-qualified than their able-bodied counterparts. One executive recruitment agency found that in executive recruitment, disabled individuals were rare and their main disadvantage was lack of experience. This was thought partly to be because some physically disabled people also suffer a degree of mental handicap which eliminates them from the majority of management jobs. More importantly, they have often been unable to take advantage of the same educational and career opportunities and so lack experience and expertise (*Nash, 1989*).

Difficult access to site

Parkside Health Authority found that one unit experienced particular problems in appointing applicants with disabilities. This was because it was situated in the country with poor public transport facilities. Also the lack of nearby schools or projects to link in with and establish work placements was a disadvantage.

Poor transport facilities was also cited as a reason why one applicant to the *Spastics Society* Graduate Training Scheme could not take up a place because it was not possible to make the move to London (*Martin, 1991*).

Existing premises

Several organisations cited problems of making alterations to existing buildings, particularly in old premises. *Anglia Television's* premises in Norwich are historic buildings and the company has had difficulties in gaining permission to make structural alterations (*IDS, 1992*).

Forward planning

At *Brent Borough Council* the Disabilities Adviser felt that the greatest problem was the lack of forward planning. Many of the initiatives are fairly long term and were difficult to carry through because other priorities interrupted them. This produces a management culture of working from day to day. This is probably prevalent in the present environment of financial cut backs and recession (*Pilling, 1992*).

Attitudes of existing staff/manager

Nottingham City Council's Equal Opportunities Training Officer considered that the biggest problem to overcome is other peoples' prejudice and building peoples' awareness of the problems (*Pilling, 1992*).

Parkside Health Authority found that in some cases work experience provision was resisted because managers found it difficult to make the leap from seeing disabled people as clients to seeing them as colleagues (*Parkside Health Authority, 1992*). They also found it difficult to get some managers to attend awareness sessions although it was not indicated why.

In the private sector *TSB's* Equal Opportunities manager argued that a key problem was in convincing people that disability was a business issue. Once it is possible to talk in terms of economic improvement and a costing of the policy can be achieved, many of the criticisms of equal opportunities policy disappear. It is no longer a purely moralistic issue (*Pilling, 1990*).

7. Reasons for Employer Inactivity on Disability Issues

This presents quite a difficult area to assess since it is unlikely that employers will readily admit to being prejudiced about people with disabilities or give the reasons why. There is therefore very little data available from employers themselves. The IFF survey asked employers if they faced any problems with employing people with disabilities (see previous section) but it is not clear whether this refers to experienced or just perceived problems.

When experiences of people with disabilities are examined it becomes clear that most problems they face arise from employer attitudes (*Thomas, 1992*). A general lack of understanding regarding the employment of people with disabilities gives rise to numerous myths and fears creating prejudice and discrimination (*Kettle, 1979; Smith, 1992; Lester & Caudill, 1987; Bolton & Roessler, 1985*).

Many employers fail to appreciate that disability does not necessarily imply inability. As indicated above (Section 2.1), a disability may not necessarily result in a handicap (*Kettle, 1979*). This lack of understanding was clearly illustrated in a small survey of 15 establishments which aimed to gauge the general disposition of employers to the recruitment of people with disabilities (*Ingamells, Rouse & Worsfold, 1991*). It was found that only a limited distinction was made between handicap and disability. Very few appeared to be aware of the wide range of disabilities, most understanding it to mean mental or physical, excluding sensory disabilities and having very little detailed knowledge of specific conditions such as cerebral palsy.

As a result managers assumed that people with disabilities would not perform adequately at work. People with disabilities were seen as 'not as capable' or not 'as mentally alert'. They were regarded as inadequate because 'we have to run up and down here' or 'they couldn't be expected to do their job properly'. Other respondents had low expectations and employed people with disabilities only in lower skilled jobs (*Ingamells, Rouse & Worsfold, 1991*). *Graham et al., (1990)* in a study of discrimination against disabled people within the workplace, found frequent examples of employers making inaccurate assumptions regarding an applicant's ability to do a job simply from an application form which stated they were disabled but had experienced no restrictions in their working life.

This poor grasp of what disability actually means leads to a whole range of specific myths and prejudices relating to employing people with disabilities. *Lester and Caudill (1987)* identified seven myths regarding the handicapped worker, some of which are supported by evidence from case studies.

1. The most frequent belief regarding people with disabilities is that they will have a poor attendance record and a high rate of job turnover.

2. It is often believed that workers with disabilities will be less productive than other employees in similar jobs because of their physical and mental limitations (contradicted by the evidence from several case-studies: *eg Du Pont, 1990*).

3. Employees with disabilities are thought to be more accident prone. This could well jeopardise an organisation's safety record and cause increased insurance premiums. This was one of the main worries expressed by managers of the Frisch food chain before they began employing people with disabilities (*PM Plus, 1992*).

4. As mentioned above, managers often do not understand how little needs to be done to accommodate an employee with a disability, assuming that very costly adjustments are necessary to the work environment. They seem to be unaware that technology is available at relatively low cost and that government grants are provided to help cover costs of accommodations (*Duckworth, 1991*). Employers consistently claim the reason for not employing people with disabilities is that they have an unsuitable work environment (*Barnes, 1991; Graham et al., 1990*).

5. Employers may claim that employees with disabilities are too demanding. Some feel that the special treatment that they require creates hostility in colleagues.

6. It is often felt that employees with disabilities would be an embarrassment to the organisation. Managers' discomfort with disability caused by their own misconceptions are assumed to be shared by customers. In one study, evidence was found that employers in the service sector felt that the sight of a disabled woman disturbed customers (*Barnes, 1990*). In addition a great deal of importance is placed on appearance. Often job advertisements require applicants to be 'generally of good appearance'. As Barnes points out, this can be very difficult for people with disabilities partly because they often can not afford clothes that satisfy this requirement, but also because manufacturers cater for the mass market which does not encompass their possible special needs.

7. Finally, it is often claimed that people with disabilities will not fit in with the organisation's work groups. One employer claimed that the simple presence of a person with a disability is disruptive to other workers in a team because of the feeling of unease and embarrassment they create in others (*Graham et al., 1990*).

All these misconceptions have proved false in both the case-studies (*eg Du Pont, 1990*) and in various research projects going back as early as 1929 (*Kettle, 1979*). Surveys of individuals such as that by the SCPR (*Prescott-Clarke, 1990*) show that the majority of disabled people in work require little more than other employees in terms of breaks or time off for treatment or sickness. This is confirmed by the IFF survey where employers who already employed people with disabilities were asked to compare their attendance record and level of performance with other employees. Sixty nine per cent of employers found the level of performance of people with disabilities the same as other workers, ten per cent found they were better and 11 per cent said they were slightly worse. On attendance record, 59 per cent of employers said people with disabilities were the same, 23 per cent had more time off and 14 per cent less (*Morrell, 1990*).

Kettle argues that the persistence of these misconceptions is not entirely the fault of employers. The medical fraternity has tended to be over-cautious regarding the abilities of people with disabilities. In interviews with individuals who had given up work because of their disability, Thomas found one of the main reasons for this was that their GPs had told them that they would never work again, without considering the possibility of working in a changed environment (*Thomas, 1992*). Such attitudes from acknowledged 'experts' can only serve to reinforce the employer's already negative feelings (*Barnes, 1991*).

In addition, until recently, most discussion regarding disability had come from the fields of medicine, rehabilitation, sociology and psychology. As Kettle points out, this is not likely to form part of a manager's daily reading. It has also not been a high priority area for management publications, and so evidence to dispel these myths would not be seen by management staff (*Kettle, 1979*).

It could be argued that the Disablement Advisory Service is attempting to overcome this lack of awareness, and in larger organisations this is very possibly the case. The IFF survey showed however, that of all private sector establishments participating, only 22 per cent had been contacted by DAS. The majority of employers, therefore, will have had fairly limited or no exposure to issues concerning employees with disabilities and no reason to re-assess their attitudes towards them.

As well as these forms of specific discrimination, many organisations have recruiting practices which inadvertently block people with disabilities from obtaining employment (*Barnes, 1991*).

Employers often have job requirements which are too tightly drawn for the actual tasks required and these tend to disadvantage people with disabilities more than other applicants. For example, the IFF survey found that 41 per cent of employers felt that management jobs required the ability to walk over half a mile (*Morrell, 1990*).

More specifically, requirements regarding educational achievements, applicant's age and experience all work against people with disabilities (*Barnes, 1990*). People with disabilities are less likely to have had the same education experiences which equip individuals with the abilities to deal with application forms, aptitude tests and interviews as well as opportunities for achieving the paper qualifications which have become increasingly important. The SCPR study found that 46 per cent of economically active people with disabilities had no qualifications (see Section 2.2) (*Prescott-Clarke, 1990*).

Many employers do not like to employ workers who are over a certain age. This presents a problem for people with disabilities because the incidence of impairments tends to increase with age (*Martin, Meltzer & Elliot, 1988*). They not only have to deal with negative attitudes towards their handicap but also regarding their age.

A great deal of importance is placed on an applicant's work experience. It is generally accepted that employers are unlikely to consider any individual who has been out of work for a year or more (*Barnes, 1990*). People with disabilities appear to experience longer periods of unemployment than the workforce as a whole. The SCPR survey found that of those actively seeking work, 52 per cent had been looking for at least a year and 30 per cent for more than three years. Although figures for the workforce as a whole are not directly comparable since they are based on those eligible to claim benefit, of these only 38 per cent had been claiming for at least a year and 19 per cent for over three years (*Prescott-Clarke, 1990*). Added to this is the disadvantage that individuals with disabilities since birth will have had limited opportunities to gain any work experience (*Prescott-Clarke, 1990*).

Although not openly acknowledged, employers fail to provide opportunities for people with disabilities partly because of their own prejudices and misunderstandings but also because of their traditional recruitment practices. Unless they can be persuaded to alter their views and recruitment procedures, it is argued, employers will continue to be unable to understand the value of employees with disabilities and will not consider them for employment (*Duckworth, 1993*).

Bibliography

Bone M and Meltzer H, 1989, *OPCS Report 3, The Prevalence of Disability among Children*, London, HMSO.

BIFU, 1992, *Breaking Down Barriers*, London, BIFU.

BIFU, 1987, *Opening Doors — A report by BIFU Disablement Advisory Committee*, London, BIFU.

Birkett K and Worman D, 1988, *Getting on with Disabilities — An Employer's Guide*, London, Institute of Personnel Management.

Bolton B and Richard Roessler R, 1985, 'After the Interview: How Employers Rate Handicapped Employees', *Personnel (USA)*, July 1985, pp. 38–41.

British Diabetic Association, 1990, *Employing people who have diabetes — Some Questions Answered*, London, British Diabetic Association.

British Diabetic Association, 1991, *Fact Sheet*, London, British Diabetic Association.

CBI, 1991, *Employment and Disabilities: A CBI View*, Confederation of British Industry Employment Affairs Report.

CBI, 1983, *Employing Disabled People*, CBI, London.

Cystic Fibrosis Research Trust, 1989, *Employer's Guide to Cystic Fibrosis*, Cystic Fibrosis Research Trust.

Dalley G (ed.), 1991, *Disability and Social Policy*, London, Policy Studies Institute.

Du Pont, 1990, *Equal to the Task II; 1990 Du Pont Survey of Employment of People with Disabilities*, Wilmington, Du Pont Corporation.

Employment Department, 1990, *Employment and Training for People with Disabilities: Consultative Document*, Employment Department, London, HMSO.

Employment Department, 1992, 'LEB gets even fitter for work', *Employment Gazette*, April 1990, p. 228.

Employment Department, 1989, *Building on Ability*, Employment Department, Sheffield (revised 1990, 1993).

Employment Service, 1990, *Code of Good Practice on the employment of disabled people*, Sheffield, Employment Service.

Employment Service, *Blind and Visually Impaired — Employing People with Disabilities Series*, Employment Service.

Employment Service, *Deaf and Hearing Impaired — Employing People with Disabilities Series*, Employment Service.

Employment Service, *Epilepsy — Employing People with Disabilities Series*, Employment Service.

Employment Service, *Haemophilia — Employing People with Disabilities Series*, Employment Service.

Employment Service, *Mental Handicap — Employing People with Disabilities Series*, Employment Service.

Employment Service, *Mental Illness — Employing People with Disabilities Series*, Employment Service.

Employment Service, *Multiple Sclerosis — Employing People with Disabilities Series*, Employment Service.

Equal Employment Opportunity Commission, 1991, 'Equal Employment Opportunity for Individuals with disabilities; Notice of Proposed Rulemaking', *Federal Register (USA)*, Vol. 56 No. 40 Part VI, February 28 1991.

Erne C, 1991, *Employment of Disabled People in Local Authorities*, London, RADAR.

Fewster C, 'The Signs of Silence', *Personnel Today (UK)*, 8–12 October 1991, pp. 30–31.

Gledhill N, 1989, 'Only People with Disabilities Need Apply', *Equal Opportunities Review*, No. 23, January/February 1989, pp. 22–25.

Graham P, Jordan J, Lamb B, 1990, *An Equal Chance? — Or No Chance?*, London, The Spastics Society.

Hansard, 1990, 21 March 1990, (Col. 607).

Haemophilia Society, The, 1991, *Introducing Haemophilia*, London, The Haemophilia Society.

Hewitson—Ratcliffe C, 1990, *Disability, Employment and Training: Meeting the Demographic Challenge of the 1990s*.

Ingamells W, Rouse S and Worsfold P, 1991, 'Employment of the disabled in the hotel and catering industry: assumptions and realities', *International Journal of Hospitality Management (UK)*, Vol. 10 No. 3, 1991, pp. 279–287.

Industrial Relations Services (IRS), 1990, 'Employing People with Disabilities 2: Policies and Practices of Employers and Trade Unions', *Industrial Relations Review and Report*, Vol. 473, 5 October 1990, pp. 10–14.

Johnson S, 1992, 'TECs and the Training of People with Disabilities: Threats and Opportunities', *Personnel Review*, Vol. 21 No. 6, 1992, pp. 5–18.

Kettle M, 1979, *Disabled People and their Employment*, Association of Disabled Professionals.

Laabs J, 1991, 'The Golden Arches Provide Golden Opportunities', *Personnel Journal (USA)*, Vol. 70 No. 7, July 1991, pp. 52–27.

Lester R and Caudill D, 1987, 'The Handicapped Worker: Seven Myths', *Training and Development Journal (USA)*, August 1987, pp. 50–51.

Martin D, 1992 'Sound Thinking', *Personnel Today (UK)*, 5 March 1991, pp. 39–40.

Martin J, Meltzer H, Elliot D, 1988, *OPCS Report 1, The Prevalence of Disability among Adults*, London HMSO.

Martin J and White A, 1988, *OPCS Report 2, The Financial Circumstances of Disabled Adults living in Private Households*, London, HMSO.

Martin J, White A, Meltzer H, 1989, *Report 4, Disabled Adults: Services, Transport and Employment*, London HMSO.

Meltzer H, Smyth M and Robus N, 1989, *OPCS Report 6, Disabled Children: Services, Transport and Education*, London, HMSO.

Morgan D, 1992 'Making People Count', *Personnel Today*, 11 February 1992, pp. 27.

Morrell J, 1990, *The Employment of People with Disabilities: Research into the policies and practices of employers — Research Paper No. 77*, IFF Research Ltd.

NALGO, *More Than Ramps*, London, Nalgo.

Nash T, 1989, 'Working Plan for the Disabled', *Director (UK)*, February, pp. 4, 5, 58 & 59.

OPCS, 1992, '1991 Census: Great Britain', OPCS: *National Monitor*, CEN 91 CM 56, December 1992.

Parkside Health Authority, 1992, *A review of Parkside's role as the NHS pilot on employing disabled people*, Parkside Health Authority.

Pilling D, Chaplin J, Floyd M, Povall M, Smith B, 1992, *Employers Actions on Disability — Case Studies*, London, Rehabilitation Resource Centre, City University.

PM Plus, 1992, 'Support for the Disabled in Two Acts', *PM Plus*, Vol. 3 No. 7, July 1992, p. 22.

PM Plus, 1991, 'Catering for People with Disabilities', *PM Plus*, Vol. 2 No. 11, November 1991, pp. 20–21.

Prescott—Clarke P, 1990, *Employment and Handicap*, London, Social and Community Planning Research.

Rumbol A, 1988, 'Numbers of Handicapped People in the Labour Market', *Research and Evaluation Branch Report No. 4*, The Employment Service.

Schlesinger H, Quinn G, Gledhill N, 1988, *Making Employment Policies for Disabled People Work in Practice*, London, Lambeth ACCORD.

Simpson J, 1992, *Workability: a research project into employment and the labour market as it affects people with disabilities*, Brighton, PACT.

Smith B, 'Americans with Disabilities — That Was Then, This Is Now', *HR Focus (USA)*, July 1992, pp. 3–5.

Smith B, Chaplin J, Floyd M, Povall M, 1991, *Employers' Action on Disability — Survey Findings*, London, Rehabilitation Resource Centre, City University.

Smyth M and Robus N, 1989, *OPCS Report 5, The Financial Circumstances of Families with Disabled Children living in Private Households*, London, HMSO.

Snell N, 1992, 'Making IS Accessible', *Datamation (USA)*, May 15 1992, pp. 79–82.

SOGAT, *Workers with Disabilities: Taking away the Obstacles — A SOGAT Guide to Action*, Rochdale, SOGAT.

Taylor S, 1990, 'Local Authority Attitudes to the Sheltered Placement Scheme', *Research and Evaluation Branch Report No. 60*, Employment Service.

Training Agency, 1989, *Building on Ability: A guide for training people with disabilities*, Researched by Deborah Cooper, Director of Skill — National Bureau for Students with Disabilities, and prepared in association with the Training Agency. Sheffield.

TUC, 1990, *Employment Department Consultative Document 'Employment and Training for People with Disabilities' — TUC Response*, London.

TUC, 1985, *TUC guide on the employment of disabled people*, TUC, London (reprinted 1989).

Tucker S, 1992, 'Mainstreaming Employees Who Have Disabilities', *Personnel Journal (USA)*, Vol. 71 No. 8, August 1992, pp. 42–49.

Institute of Manpower Studies